Distributed by
Nataraj Books
P.O. Box 5076
Springfield, VA 22150

SOVIET ECONOMY
NEW ECONOMIC STRATEGY

Soviet Economy
New Economic Strategy

Vinod Mehta

STERLING PUBLISHERS PRIVATE LIMITED

STERLING PUBLISHERS PRIVATE LIMITED
L-10, Green Park Extension, New Delhi-110016
24, Race Course Road, Bangalore-560001.

Soviet Economy: New Economic Strategy

PRINTED IN INDIA
Published by S.K. Ghai, Managing Director, Sterling Publishers Private Limited, L-10, Green Park Extension, New Delhi-110016.

PREFACE

The Twenty-seventh Congress of the CPSU is going to be a landmark in the economic history of the Soviet Union. The old approach to economic management which gave the Soviet Union one of the highest growth rates in the world is no longer valid. The focus of development has shifted from extensive to intensive development. Under the strategy delineated by the Twenty-seventh Congress, rigid planning will give way to flexible planning and the economy will make use of economic levers on a large scale. Moreover, the emphasis is shifting to modernisation and use of new technologies in the industrial and agricultural sectors. Along with modernisation emphasis is being placed on efficiency and responsiveness of the industry to the needs of the society at large and consumers in particular.

It is not too early to assess the possible impact of the new strategy for the economic development of the Soviet Union since some of the positive indications are already there. The decisions of the Twenty-seventh Congress have unleashed forces in the economic sphere which are likely to have a salutary effect on the economic growth of the Soviet Union. In order to understand these forces, it is essential to know the context in which these changes are being introduced. This book is a humble attempt to try to understand the new economic strategy in the context of the accumulated problems of the Soviet economy.

4th December, 1986. Vinod Mehta

CONTENTS

1

INTRODUCTION

The Twenty-seventh Congress of the Communist Party of the Soviet Union (CPSU) may well turn out to be a landmark in the economic history of the Union of Soviet Socialist Republics (USSR) or Soviet Union in short.

CPSU Central Committee General Secretary Mikhail Gorbachev's Report to the Twenty-seventh Congress of the CPSU, while praising the economic achievements of the past six decades also pointed out the shortcomings, administrative and others, which were coming in the way of realising the full economic potential of the Soviet Union. The General Secretary Gorbachev noted in his report: "For a number of years the deeds and actions of Party and Government bodies tailed behind the needs of the times and of life—not only because of the objective factors, but also for reasons above all of a subjective nature. The problems in the country's development built up more rapidly than they were being solved. The inertness and stiffness of the forms and methods of administration, the decline of dynamism in our work, and an escalation of bureaucracy—all this was doing no small damage. Signs of stagnation had begun to surface in the life of society."

Therefore, he stressed the need to overcome the negative factors which were acting as a hurdle in the rapid socio-economic development of the country. Some of these negative factors which have been identified in the report may be summarised as follows:

(a) under-utilization of existing capacities in the industries;
(b) over investment in certain industries to the detriment of other important lines of production;
(c) extravagant use of scarce raw materials;
(d) slow absorption of new technologies and innovations;
(e) lack of quality control;
(f) disregard for ecology;
(g) slow growth of the agricultural sector;

(h) bureaucratic responses to the problems of economic management.

These were fully elaborated by Gorbachev in his major speech at a meeting of the Khabarovsk Territory Party activists on July 31, 1986. He reminded the Party workers of Khabarovsk about the industrial importance of their region in the Far East and added that while the territory was rich in natural resources and had a pool of highly trained manpower, the economic results were not commensurate with its natural resources and its technical cadre.

Talking about the management of industrial units in the Khabarovsk territory, Gorbachev observed: "There has also been a decline in the share of top quality products in the general industrial output of the territory in the 11th Five Year Plan. The economic executives have grown used to a situation where consumers accept everything for lack of something better. But what about conscience in this case and the country's need for more cost-effective, reliable and higher quality products? There are many enterprises which have been putting out the same products manufactured by the same old methods for 10 or even 15 years, and not really caring. I will put it straight for you: the managers in this case should not be paid anything, since everything is done by the workers. After all, the primary responsibility of the director and of the whole managerial staff to the country is to satisfy the demand for ever new economical and reliable products meeting the highest requirements. That is where their responsibility lies."[1]

As for the under-utilization of capacities in the existing units, Gorbachev provided many concrete examples. One such example related to a Knitwear factory in Khabarovsk. To quote: "In 1975 or more than ten years ago, the Bikinskaya Knitwear factory was put into operation. However even ten years later it is running at only 40 per cent of its capacity. This means that our money there lies idle. Against the approved number of 1,240, the factory employs only 520 men or only 40 per cent of the required workforce. The principal explanation for its poor performance is the shortage of manpower and specialists. But has this transpired only now? This must have been known all along. This means that the initial design should have provided both for the construction of production facilities and for the establishment of an adequate social groundwork."[2]

Similarly, Mikhail Gorbachev expressed his concern over the development of agriculture in the Khabarovsk. To quote: "Take the problems of development of agriculture. The Central Committee is worried that you are increasing the load on state resources with every passing year. You place demands on the centre and others, but do not fulfil your plans and State orders although these orders are ensured by big investments and material technical means received by the Khabarovsk territory. Over the past five years state subsidies have increased."[3]

Through his Political Report to the Twenty-seventh Party Congress and through various forums, Mikhail Gorbachev has initiated a debate on the current economic problems so that appropriate answers could be found to meet the new challenges, of course, within the socialist framework. There is no going back to the market mechanism of the pre-revolutionary era, as interpreted by some scholars from the western countries. A careful study of his speeches would reveal that it is the man who is at the centre of attention, and economic levers will be used only to tackle the negative factors in the management of the economy. No free play of market forces is envisaged in settling the issue of alternative investment plans, or fixing the prices of essential commodities and services. It is more like using the concept of shadow prices, opportunity cost, controlled interest rates etc., to economise on resources and to achieve optimum allocation, keeping in view the tastes and wishes of the people. The managers are likely to be given relatively more freedom and encouragement, to manufacture goods in shapes, sizes and colours which the people want and to ensure that, the innovations are speedily absorbed in the industries.

This is what Mikhail Gorbachev meant when he said to the 27th Congress: "It is our task to conceptualise broadly, in Lenin's style, the times we are living in and to work out a realistic, thoroughly weighed programme of action that will organically blend the grandeur of our aims with our real capabilities, and the Party's plans with the hopes and aspirations of every person."[4]

In the chapters that follow, after dealing with the history of planning, we shall go on to discuss the directions which the Soviet economy will take following the Twelfth Plan.

References

1. Soviet Review, August 25, 1986, p. 13
2. *Ibid,* p. 14
3. *Ibid,* p. 15
4. Political Report, p. 3

2

PLANNING : A BIT OF HISTORY AND THEORY

In order to understand the changes being introduced in the economic management, it is essential to understand the history of Planning in the Soviet Union and the theory and method of planning.

It is common knowledge that the Soviet Union by overthrowing the Tsarist regime in 1917, had created the political conditions for proceeding along the path of planned economic development but the economic conditions were not as yet ripe for doing so. Nevertheless the question of embarking on this path, as soon as conditions were ripe, was under constant consideration. Lenin who led the successful October Revolution made a signal contribution to the solution of the problems of planning.

Lenin on Planning

In his numerous writings Lenin provided many scientific solutions to the key problems of the management and planning of the socialist economy. It is well known that the foundations of planned economic development were laid under the personal guidance of Lenin.

According to Lenin, a systematic organisation of social production constitutes the pivotal point in planned management. Only in a workers' state can a scientific economic plan, which reflects the interests of the workers, be implemented. A workers' government can mobilise and organise all the production resources and set the process of economic development in motion.

He visualised a single national economic plan of extended socialist reproduction, reflecting the balance and unity of inter-industry and inter-district division of labour. In 1920, Lenin wrote that "the plans of the various branches of production must be soundly coordinated and linked up so as to constitute the single economic plan we stand in such great need of."[1]

While elaborating the idea of a single economic plan, Lenin also emphasised the importance of centralised management of the economy, both technologically and economically. Without such centralisation it would be difficult to implement the plan. At another place he wrote that "... the material source, the productive source, the foundation of socialism, calls for absolute and strict unity of will, which directs the joint labours of hundreds, thousands and tens of thousands of people."[2]

Economic planning is nothing but the systematic regulation of national production. Public ownership of the means of production presupposes coordinated development of all the sectors. No single enterprise can develop in isolation from the rest of the economy. The function of regulating each component of the socialist economy, and the economy as a whole, devolves on the single economic plan. Lenin underlined this aspect when he stated that "only large-scale, planned construction, which aims at evenly utilising economic and business values, deserves to be called socialist."[3]

According to Lenin the system and methods of economic planning were very important in the regulation of economic growth. He emphasised the importance of harmony in politics and economics, scientific and realistic nature of planning and democratic centralism. He also maintained that once accepted, the economic plans must be binding, that there should be long-term planning, supervision of plan fulfilment and rational system of stock-taking, accounting and statistics.

Economic planning is meaningful when it is backed by political will. "Without a correct political approach", Lenin said, "the workers will not be able to stay at the top and will be incapable of solving economic problems." According to him an integrated economic and political approach required that political aims of improving and developing the social system should always be kept in view. He wrote that "as we begin socialist reforms, we must have a clear conception of the goal towards which these reforms are in the final analysis directed, that is, the creation of a communist society."[4]

Thus, in Lenin's view, the first step was to formulate and scientifically substantiate the political and economic aims of the main development tasks. These could be either formulated as development trends or as levels to be attained. Regarding substantiation, Lenin said that the planners should be sure "that out extensive plans... are not fantasies, but are borne out by and based on technology and science . . . "[5]

While drafting the national plans, the planners must take into account the main trends of technological progress (such as the level of automation attained in various production processes, introduction of chemistry in technological processes, electrification, etc.) and the experience of the practical activities of millions of working people. It is essential that plans are based on progressive technical economic standards so that full use of national resources is made.

Lenin also advocated rational division of labour between Republics and different areas of the country on the basis of each region's natural endowments, living conditions and national and historical features.

He also insisted on the drawing up of realistic economic plans, since a single miscalculation could damage the entire economy. Referring to the fuel difficulties of 1921, Lenin pointed out that the resources had been wrongly estimated, that nothing was left for the rainy day, although it was just impossible to run the national economy without reserves. He observed that the fuel and transport crises had been caused "not only by a shortage of material resources, but by a miscalculation of the rate of development."[6]

The principle of democratic centralism is central to the theory of planning. Building socialism, Lenin pointed out, "means building a centralised economic system directed from the centre."[7] Democratic centralism implies the existence of general industrial and territorial planning bodies, whose directives are carried out promptly and accurately by the organs lower down the line, while the apex planning bodies also consider the proposals submitted from below. This helps to create a stable and reliable economic position for each production unit, determining its position and prospects for future development in the overall division of labour. Since it is a complex system, it can be successful only if it is combined with economic independence at the enterprise level and relies on the initiative of the masses.

Lenin's idea of democratic centralism was against bureaucratic centralism and anarchy. He said, "We are for democratic centralism. . . . There is nothing more mistaken than confusing democratic centralism with bureaucracy and routinism. Our task now is to carry out democratic centralism in the economic sphere, to ensure absolute harmony and unity in the functioning of such economic undertakings as the railways, the postal and telegraph services, other means of transport, and so forth. At the same time, centralism, understood in a truly democratic sense, presupposes the possibility, created for the first time in history, of full and unhampered development not only of specific local features, but also of local inventiveness, local initiative of diverse ways, methods and means of progress to the common goal."[8]

Lenin was also in favour of long term plans. He wrote; "Do not be afraid of long-term plans, for without them you cannot achieve an economic revival. Let us devote all our energies in the localities to their fulfilment."[9] He emphasised that to create and develop the new economic system, one must have a clear perspective. While he underlined the decisive role of long-term planning, he insisted on unity between long-term and current planning. According to him, a long-term plan had to be given concrete expression in current plans, and it should be "amplified, elaborated, corrected and applied in the light of well-scrutinised practical experience."[10]

Lenin also regarded a rational system of stock-taking, accounting and statistics, and the prompt compilation of scientifically classified exact statistical data covering every area in the country and the entire economy, as essential and was particular about organising such a system. The foundations of such a system were laid on the instructions of Lenin soon after the October Revolution. The Central Statistical Board and various other local statistical bodies were set up in 1918. Similarly, the state planning body, Gosplan, was also set up on his instructions.

Lenin's ideas could be summarised as follows:

(a) *Democratic centralism* in planning which implies the integral combination of centralised planned management and maximum development of the independence and initiative of local authorities, enterprises and production work-force;

(b) *Directive planning and the use of economic levers*, i.e., a combination of strictly compulsory planning assignments and the use of prices, credit, profit and other economic levers that have a goal-directed effect on plan execution and raising the efficiency of social production;

(c) *Unity of the macro-economic plan*, meaning that all plans for different branches of production must be strictly coordinated. This principle is determined by the unity of the entire process of socialist extended reproduction;

(d) *Coordination of perspective and current plans*, in which the perspective plan incorporating the major tasks of building socialism and communism plays the leading role;

(e) *Coordination of the sectoral and regional breakdowns* for a particular plan arising from the interests of the economy taken as a whole and each region taken separately.

The most important principles underpinning work on a macro-economic plan — maintenance of a proper balance between all elements of the economy, a steady rise in the efficiency of social production and the methods of socialist planning (i.e. the balance method and the method of optional decision-making, by which proportionality with heightened efficiency of social production are attained) — have all been developed on the basis of Lenin's ideas.

Improvement of planning theory and practice calls, above all, for further development of planning and forecasting methods. Broad introduction of systems analysis and of economic mathematical models helps ensure that plans for social and economic development are complex, that a large number of factors and trends can be taken into account in analysing and evaluating planning decisions and their outcomes and that the best plan is selected for the particular concrete situation.

The Basic Principles of Setting up a Macro-economic Plan

The principles of formulating a macro-economic plan are determined by the goals of the socialist country. In order to satisfy society's continually increasing needs to the maximum extent possible, the plan must secure, firstly a steady growth of proportional, balanced social production and secondly, a rise in the efficiency of social production. These two planning principles determine the content of the plan and the process of formulating it.

The direct link that exists between production and social

needs, which has made it possible to plan production in the light of the structure and composition of those needs which society should satisfy before all others, is a cardinal feature of the socialist planning. As Engels pointed out, the objective possibility of regulating production in accordance with needs is created in conditions of socialism.

Raising the efficiency of social production constitutes another extremely important principle of planning. The efficiency principle requires plan goals to be attained with minimum inputs of materials, labour and finance.

THE SUBJECT MATTER OF PLANNING THEORY

In the course of planned socialist construction, a science of planning which is based on the methodology for ascertaining and making use of the "objective economic laws of socialism in planning", is still being developed in the Soviet Union. It has arisen from the need for scientifically validated management of the socialist economy and gives theoretical expression to the practice of planning in the Soviet Union and other socialist countries.

Planning theory works out the methodology and methods for defining the basic development indicators of a socialist economy over a perspective period and especially growth rates and proportions, methods for studying social needs and resources and ways of balancing them in the most efficient way, as well as methods for setting and achieving planning assignments and for checking on their execution.

Planning of the Soviet economy covers all spheres and sectors of the economy and all parts and aspects of reproduction. Both material production (industry, agriculture, construction, transport and communications, trade procurement of farm produce and the supply of materials and equipment) and the non-productive sphere (education, health, culture, sports, science, municipal services, amenities, etc.), both economic processes and social relations constitute the object of planning. Planning presupposes an object of planning, which is the socialist economy and a subject of planning, which in this case is the socialist state performing the role of direct organiser of the whole of social production.

The basic tasks of planning the economy comprise:

(a) assessing both production and non-production social needs with a view to meeting them as fully as possible, given the available resources;

(b) determining society's material, labour and financial resources and their most efficient allocation and use in accordance with current and long-term requirements;

(c) searching out ways of attaining high economic growth rates, while maintaining an optimal combination of growth in output and consumption;

(d) achieving a correct balance between different spheres, sectors and elements in the economy, and maintaining proportionality in economic development;

(e) securing the right technical, economic and organisational conditions for successfully fulfilling plans.

As a science, the Soviet theory of economic planning takes as its premise the basic conclusions of dialectical and historical materialism, and Marxist-Leninist economic science.

Planning theory is grounded in political economy, economic statistics and cybernetics, in the economies of the specific industries and the corresponding technical sciences, in the sum total of knowledge of all the sciences needed to provide a profound, all-round validation of economic development plans.

Political economy, which studies economic laws, provides the immediate theoretical basis for the science of planning. The latter works out the correct methodology for applying the whole system of economic laws, provides the new data for determining economic policy, and develops means of implementing it in development plans.

The political economy of socialism and the science of planning emerged and are developing simultaneously, interacting with one another and influencing each other. Thus, if the basic economic law of socialism forms the basis for determining optimality criteria in the plan, then the elaboration of these optimality criteria in turn make it possible to gain a deeper and more comprehensive understanding of the basic economic law. By giving concrete expression to the conclusions of political economy regarding planning tasks in each particular planned period, by checking them out in the course of generalising the experience of planned management of the economy in theory, planning science presents political economy with new tasks. The development of political economy helps raise the scientific level of planning and makes it easier to tackle the tasks facing it with regard to improving planning methods, the price system, economic motivation, methods for increasing the efficiency of social production and so on.

Planning is closely connected with particular economic sectors. Thus, for example, planning theory studies the regularities that shape the organisational forms taken by the socialisation of labour concentration, specialisation and the combination of production in different branches of industry, agriculture and in other sectors of material production, especially when problems affecting sectoral structure and inter-sectoral linkages are being worked out.

There is a similar tie-up between planning theory and statistics. Analysis of the initial plan level relies completely on methods of statistical analysis, basic indicators of economic development, and the data of annual report balances. It should be noted that statistics at present primarily perform checking and purely accounting functions, working on the individual indicators of separate enterprises. The system of statistical indicators still lags behind the growing need for deep economic analysis, especially the dynamics of economic processes at the macro-economic and inter-sectoral level.

Planning theory broadly uses methods of economic mathematical modelling. They were first used in practice at the preplanning stage, but they are now being used increasingly in the actual compilation of a plan.

Inter-sectoral models, multiple-factor models of economic growth, models depicting the structure of personal consumption, and sectoral optimisation models are among those that are most highly developed. Further work is being done on improving these models with a view to constructing an interconnected system of planning models which will enable work to be done on optimisation of the whole of the national economic plan.

Optimal sectoral models of production and regional location have been widely accepted for planning the development of economic sectors. The use of these models in practice is already achieving a tremendous economic impact.

Planning is the central link or core in managing an economy since it is linked with the science of organising economic management. The general theory of management includes planning as the most important function of the management.

THE JOB OF PLANNING THEORY AND PRACTICE

Improvement of management in accordance with a dynamically developing economy has been of late an important plank of the CPSU's economic policy. Measures to improve the direction of the economy are considered as one of the main reserves whose use will help in the Twelfth Five-Year Plan and getting results in the immediate future.

The main tasks of macro-economic planning at the present stage of development of the economy are accurate study of social needs; scientific forecasts and estimates of economic possibilities and reserves; all-round analysis and appraisal of the different variants of solutions; real evaluation of the immediate and long-term consequence of the planning decisions taken.

It is necessary in the first place to ensure closer combination of long-term, Five-Year and current plans. A feature of the Twelfth Five Year Plan is that it was prepared simultaneously with the drafting of the basic principles for the country's developments during the longer period ending in 2000 A.D. The Central planning authorities, in future, will have to complete the drafting of the long-term programmes and concrete targets, jointly with the scientific organizations.

A long-term development plan should reflect the objective laws of laying the material and technical base of communism; it should contain a formulation of the most important social, economic, scientific and technical tasks and the main ways of tackling them, a description of the basic elements of economic growth and inter-sectoral proportions, and technical and economic assessment of future development particularly in sectoral and regional complexes.

The two basic principles of setting up a plan are closely

interwoven. Society's need for fuel can, for example, be satisfied in large measure by the use of coal, peat, etc. If this is done, a correct balance of resource and needs will be achieved, but it will not be efficient. If balance is achieved with the use of inefficient types of fuel, the whole system of proportions deteriorates, a brake is put on economic development and there are fewer opportunities for satisfying people's needs. If the share of gas and oil in the fuel balance is increased, then it becomes possible to meet society's requirements with fewer inputs. It is also possible to satisfy society's food requirements by disproportionately increasing the output of bread, potatoes and other foods of low nutritional value. This requires relatively small inputs of labour but it wll not correspond to people's needs. Such a solution would destroy the proportion between needs and production in its structural breakdown.

Improvement of the structure of social production and raising of its efficiency have been provided for, at all stages of Soviet perspective plans. This has been reflected in progressive changes in the structure of the fuel balance and accelerated development of electricity generation. The branches of the chemical industry, progressive branches of engineering, and other industries have shown marked development, thereby ensuring scientific and technical progress.

The structure of social production has improved through singling out the leading sectors and there has been improvement in efficiency at all stages of building socialism. In conditions of centralised planning, society concentrates on all types of resources (production, investment, manpower, etc.) and allocates them for developing key sectors and tackling the most important social problems.

It should however, be noted that, although the Soviet plans, on the whole do achieve a proper balance, the question of improving the efficiency of social production has not yet been altogether satisfactorily solved.

Emergence of Gosplan as Planning Body

Throughout the 1920s, a number of agencies dealt with the planning problems. These included, among others, Vesenkha (VSNH), the supreme body for peoples economy, the People's Commissariat of Finance, the People's Commissariat of Transportation, Gosplan and various regional bodies. However, it was Gosplan which was exclusively concerned with economic planning. The decree of 1922 specifically stated that Gosplan's duties were "the preparation not only of a long-range plan but also of an operational plan for the current year."

The Gosplan made a modest beginning in this direction in 1921. In 1925, it had around 50 economists and statisticians on its staff. But by the late 1920s it came to be accepted as the planning agency in charge of coordinating economic plans for the entire economy. What enabled it to emerge as the premier planning body, was its work on the annual *control figures* (or tentative output targets) for various branches of the economy. Its first control figures were prepared for the year 1925-26. Though initially the figures did not prove important yet they were used to establish the principle that from then on, the economic policy should be framed on an annual basis on the basis of control figures prepared by the Gosplan. Thus the Gosplan came to play a supervisory role in the preparation of plans by other administrative bodies. Though its role as coordinator of all planning work was developing, it had little to do with the actual operational planning of the economy. The actual planning work was done by VSNH and its Glavki (Central board). In 1925 VSNH was instructed to prepare production and financial plans on the basis of Gosplan's 1925-1926 control figures. In 1926-27, the production and financial plans of VSNH were scrutinised by the Gosplan and the Commissariat of Finance.

In 1925, when the shortage of basic industrial commodities grew and the administrative allocation of such commodities increased, the planning bodies started compiling balances for critical industrial materials. Out of this grew the system of material balances which is widely used in physical planning. This system was first used in the iron-and-steel industry and then in fuel. In 1928, this system was extended to the building materials industry. Both VSNH and Gosplan were in charge of coordinating the balance on the basis of production and financial plans and control figures.

Planning on a country-wide scale began in 1928 with the adoption of the First Five Year Plan based on the following planning principles. Firstly, the Gosplan was to be the central coordinating authority to which all other planning bodies were to submit proposals. Secondly, the control figures prepared by the Gosplan were to guide the economy on an annual basis. Thirdly, the detailed operational production and financial plans of enterprises were to conform to the control figures prepared by the Gosplan. Finally, the materials were to be allocated through the system of balances which were compiled from the control figures and production and financial plans of enterprises.

Gosplan became the central planning body in 1932, when the ministerial system was also introduced. Between 1928 and 1932, the functions of VSNH had grown increasingly complex. This coordinating body for industry, was dissolved in 1932. Its sub-departments known as Glavket became accordingly Peoples' Commissariat, in charge of planning and administration of their enterprises.

Another important feature introduced into the planning system during the First Five Year Plan period was centralised administration in regard to the setting of prices, which proved a very complex task. Though during the NEP (New Economic Policy) period the setting of prices was largely decentralised, the VSNH and the Commission for Internal Trade gained increasing authority towards the end of this period. This tendency became more pronounced after the introduction of comprehensive planning in 1928. Not only were the domestic prices protected from foreign influence through monopoly in foreign trade but the pricing system itself was used to achieve desired results.

After having dealt with the history and theory of planning, we now come to the actual practice of planning and investment in the Soviet Union.

Property Structure

For a proper understanding of the economic processes going on in any country and the character of the various economic institutions and policies, it is, first of all, essential to know the property structure of that country. Investment and production decisions and fiscal, monetary, incomes and pricing policies are directly related to the property structure obtaining in a country. In a capitalist economy, the means of production are owned by the capitalists who alone make investment decision, taking their cue from the pricing and profit trends of various commodities. The driving force of production is the pursuit of personal profit. Production is not for the satisfaction of demands of the population at large but for those who can afford to pay. Similarly, where private property as the means of production rules the roost, the incomes and pricing policies have very rarely succeeded. Again the labour laws as they obtain in the capitalist countries have to function within the private-property framework.

Property in the Soviet Union

In the Soviet Union, a distinction is made between the ownership of means of production and ownership of consumer goods. The Soviet laws allow an individual to own only consumer goods such as furniture, clothes, TV sets, radios, motorcycles, cars etc., which directly satisfy the demands of consumers. Unlike in the capitalist countries, the individuals cannot own producer goods or means of production. There is public ownership of the means of production.

In the Soviet Union there are two forms of public ownership *state property* (belonging to the people as a whole), and *cooperative property* (belonging to a group of people, such as a collective farm). Since in a socialist society, the means of production belong to the people as a whole, and their interests are vested in the state, public property is also referred to as state property.

Public or *state ownership* is the main form of socialist ownership. It implies that all the main tools and means of production, as well as output, belong to the society as a whole, to all the working people.

State socialist property includes land, its mineral wealth, waters, forests, factories, mines, all means of transport and communications, houses in towns and urban-type settlements as well as the greater part of cultural and art establishments. In the Soviet Union, 92 per cent of the means of production are state property. Eighty per cent of all those engaged in the national economy, work at state enterprises.[11]

Cooperative property is the property of the individual collective farms and cooperative associations. Unlike public (state) property, it does not belong to the people as a whole. It is a form of group property. The members of a collective farm, work on their land jointly, using means of production that are jointly owned. The land, they till, is public property and is turned over to them by the State for their perpetual and free use.

Cooperative property includes farm tools and machinery, farm power stations, farm buildings and cultural and communal buildings, such factories as a farm may need to process its produce, livestock and the output of the farm. Collective-farm property in the Soviet Union accounts for seven per cent of the country's basic production assets.[12]

Thus when the means of production are owned by the Society, the driving force of production is not private profit but the satisfaction of the demands of the public. One is likely to point out here that in the Soviet Union, the enterprises also earn profits. We may clarify at the outset that profit as an economic category does exist in the Soviet Union, but it is not a driving force of production. The managers and directors of an enterprise do not appropriate the profits and they do not make investment and pricing policy decisions. Profits in the Soviet Union are generally the difference between the price of a product as stipulated by the planning authorities and cost reduction achieved by an enterprise through better use of raw materials and the economy effected in the use of fuels. In a sense, the profit of an enterprise in the Soviet Union is a device to see that the enterprise is run efficiently and the resources are not frittered away.

Similarly, the public ownership of the means of production also allows pursuit of meaningful incomes and pricing policies. In other words, the ownership of means of production determines the nature of economic institutions and economic policies and has a bearing on the life of a society as a whole.

Planning and Investment

In the Soviet Union, all important economic decisions, such as the allocation of output for consumption, investment and defence, and the rates of growth of different sectors of the economy are made administratively and not by the market. These most basic economic decisions are made by the Communist Party of the Soviet Union (CPSU) and the Supreme Soviet of the USSR. The Gosplan (the planning apparatus in the Soviet Union which is a branch of the state government) then draws up a plan for all sectors of the economy which implement these basic political and economic decisions. The state planning body has to perform five tasks.

First, to determine the criteria of economic calculations underlying the planning period.

Second, to determine and quantify the targets to be achieved in the planning period.

Third, to coordinate the targets so as to ensure the internal consistency of the plan.

Fourth, to determine appropriate methods to ensure plan fulfilment.

Fifth, to revise the targets according to the changing conditions.

Planning is a complex and difficult task. Many things have to be reconciled administratively. A polish economist defines planning as a "....... system of managing economic processes involving production, distribution, investment and consumption. Its essence consists in determining economic targets and methods for their implementation, in particular the allocation of the means of production and of labour to different uses. As such, planning is an instrument of economic strategy to achieve the optimum growth of national income or the maximum satisfaction of social needs."[13]

Since 1928, the Gosplan had been handling the difficult task of planning. In the course of time, it has introduced many important refinements.

Aims of Planning

The ultimate goal of economic and social planning in the Soviet Union is to build a communist society. But it is recognised that to achieve this goal a number of stages must be gone through. The principal goals and main tasks facing the Soviet Union at each stage of its development are defined in long-term and current national economic plans.

In the USSR there are three types of plans: long-term, medium-term (five years) and current (annual) plans. The Twelfth Plan is a part of the long-term perspective plan which covers the period upto the year 2000.

The necessity of long-term plan arises from the fact that the Soviet Union has reached a high level of economic development and has to accomplish new scientific, technological, economic and socio-political tasks. A perspective plan is needed to tackle such problems as the abundant provision of consumer goods and services for the complete satisfaction of the people's material and spiritual needs, as well as such scientific, technical and production problems as the creation of a nuclear power industry, the development of large territorial production complexes, the southward diversion of waters from the great Siberian rivers to the Central Asian deserts, etc.

Before such long-term plans are drafted, intensive work is done on forecasting the country's development over a long period, say, 15 to 20 or even to 30 years. Forecasts for the first 15 years are exceptionally detailed but are more general for the later years.

A perspective or long-range forecast includes a forecast of the development and application of science and technology, forecast of social change under mature socialism with its rising level of cultural and educational standards, expansion of health services, changes in working and living conditions and improvements in the management of the economy.

The potential for economic growth is determined by forecasting exploitable natural resources and their use in production. Plans are drawn up for their better use.

A new aspect of long-range planning is the forecasting of the expansion of the Soviet Union's economic ties with foreign countries. For instance, the comprehensive programme of economic integration has charted the development of ties among the CMEA (Council for the Mutual Economic Assistance) countries for 15 to 20 years. In the recent past the Soviet Union's economic relations with the West-European countries, Japan and the USA have grown substantially. The long-term trade and other economic agreements with them, determine the further sizeable expansion of economic cooperation between the USSR and the capitalist countries.

Finally, a demographic forecast is made which estimates population growth and change in its composition according to sex and age, the natural birth rate, the size and structure of the able-bodied population, etc.

The forecast of economic growth is based on the forecasts enumerated above.

It should be noted that a long-range economic forecast is not a plan because in the Soviet Union a plan is a directive which is binding on a particular enterprise or institution. A long-range forecast simply defines the trend and the main growth parameters for particular sectors and the establishment of major territorial production complexes. It only indicates the trends of economic and social development and the approximate levels to be reached in each five-year period of the forecast as regards the growth of the social product, national income, major production items, investments and personal consumption.

In the Soviet Union, the scientific long-range forecast is only a prelude to the drafting of a Five-Year plan. According to Soviet economists it is difficult to prepare a Five-Year plan without having some idea of development over the ensuing 10 or 15 years.

Apart from macro-economic forecasts, sector-wise forecasts, particularly those which are decisive for speeding up technological progress and for raising the living standards of the people, are widely used in the Soviet Union. Among them are long-term plans for the development of power industry, electronics, chemical, ferrous, non-ferrous and rare-metals industries as well as the improvement of land and the integration of national transport in a single network.

The growth prospects of the Union Republics and economic regions are minutely considered for the drawing up of long-range forecasts. While each Union Republic, territory and administrative region specialises at the all-Union level in one or more branches of production, each economic region has to be comprehensively developed in all sectors of production, with a correct combination of all branches of material production, both major and auxiliary, and social and cultural development. For instance, a long-term plan for 1976-90 has been drawn up for seven major economic regions; three regions in the European part of the USSR (namely Northern, Central and Southern), Siberia, Central Asia, Kazakhstan and the Far East.

The planning of large territorial production complexes of national importance has developed a great deal in these regions. A few projects have already been undertaken. For instance, the Sayany-Shushenkoye complex in East Siberia will have, besides the world's largest hydro-electric power station, timber mills and aluminium works, fertiliser plants and heavy engineering, food-processing and light industry enterprises. An agro-industrial production complex is also being developed. The 1976-90 plan also envisages the establishment of such big multi-sectoral complexes in different economic territories.

The medium-term plan or the five-year plan is the basic type of national economic plan in the Soviet Union. The long-term plan only outlines the developmental trends and simply indicates parameters; the Five-Year-Plan, on the other hand, broken down into annual plans, is essentially an *operational* plan.

The basic five-year plan sets the main production targets for all the sectors, ministries, ministerial departments and Union Republics, determines the scale of investments and the main proportions of social production and fixes principal assignments in the social and cultural fields and for raising the living standards of the people.

A full range of economic indicators are used while drafting the Five-Year-Plan. These indicators in turn are drawn on the basis of the perspective plan. The Five-Year Plan is then broken up into current, short-term, annual plan.

At the operational level, every enterprise has its own five-year plan as well as fixed norms for the same period and technical development plans. Enterprises have all the necessary conditions for their steady and uninterrupted operation. These plans define what goods, the enterprises are expected to produce in the five-year period and at what prices; what planned and above-plan profits they will be able to make and what funds they will have for the payment of wages and material incentives and for expanding production.

Planning becomes more detailed when annual plans are drawn up on the basis of the Five-Year Plan. If the circumstances warrant, the plan is amended in the course of its fulfilment because during that period new needs may arise or spare capacity may be discovered. It is also possible that new foreign commitment may be undertaken or there may be another drought.

Guiding Principles for Drafting Plans

The Soviet planning bodies, while drafting the plans, are guided by two main and closely related considerations. The first is to raise the efficiency of social production and the second to ensure the balanced development of the economy.

A high degree of efficiency is possible only if there is balanced and proportionate growth. This implies that the structural balance of the economy must be achieved not at any cost, irrespective of the expenditure, but at a minimal unit cost. This is possible only if the plan is based on the maximum application of scientific and technological innovations, and it makes the maximum use of enterprises' potentialities and a proper allocation of investments, output, prices, wages, etc. Soviet experience shows that high growth rates in social production and social consumption help synchronise high growth rates of consumption and accumulation. The high growth rates, in turn, are a function of the rational use of productive capacities, natural resources and manpower, proper concentration of investments, etc.

Since 1965 the Soviet Union has introduced reforms to stimulate the economy. One of the most significant measures relates to the system of enterprise funds which include the material incentives fund for workers, the fund for social and cultural amenities and housing for workers and the production development fund. The first two funds are used by the enterprise for the benefit of the workers while the third is used for expanding production, etc. The enterprise funds are larger when more output is sold and more profits are made. This incentive stimulates the workers to bring to the fore, the hidden potentialities of an enterprise.

Under the new system if an enterprise exceeds the five-year plan targets for a given year, it may make additions to the material incentives fund. For instance, during the Ninth Plan, a textile mill was to sell goods worth 100 million roubles in 1973. Out of this 20 percent of the resulting income was earmarked for payment of wages. But after the 1969 financial year it was found that the workers had produced goods worth 110 million roubles without any increase in the labour force. This implied that the wage bill would rise from 20 to 22 million roubles and the average wage by 10 per cent as compared with the original plan. The benefits that accrued from over-fulfilment were twofold; the consumers received 10 million roubles worth of more fabrics and the workers earned 10 per cent more wages.[14]

As Professor Braginsky points out, "Since in the Soviet Union the basic indicators of the enterprise (association) plan have to be endorsed, the higher body checks the tightness of these plans, the main criterion being the use made of available productive capacity, raw materials and the working day. The previous example demonstrated that the textile mills undertook to increase output on a scale bigger than projected by the ministry and to do so without any centralised investments and in some cases with reduction in the number of workers. This is an example of a fairly tight plan under which an increase in the volume of production is achieved by the use of intensive factors of economic growth. For new enterprises and new units *in old enterprises* the criterion of tightness is the level of utilisation of production capacity. In general, efficieny is the principal criterion."[15]

Thus the chief aim of planning in the Soviet Union is to raise the standard of living of the people by achieving maximum output with minimum input. The optimal economic plan aims at coordinating the various factors so as to ensure high and stable rate of growth of production, accumulation and consumption.

Steps in the Formulation of an Actual Plan

The first step in the planning process is for the Party to formulate priorities for the forthcoming planning period. This is normally done in the spring, preceding the planning period. The Party generally determines the priorities by setting output targets in the form of desired rates of growth for a number of crucial commodities.

The second step is to send these targets to the Gosplan which has been gathering data on the fulfilment of the previous plan and the bottlenecks found therein. On the basis of these data, the Gosplan formulates a preliminary set of control figures (tentative output targets) for about 300 product groups in line with the priorities set by the Party. It also makes tentative estimates, on the basis of past performance, of inputs required to achieve these control figures. At this stage, the planning departments of various ministries assist the Gosplan in working out control figures and projecting input requirements.

The third step involves the sending of these control figures through the planning hierarchy, via the ministerial organisations, to individual enterprises. As the figures go down to the individual enterprise, they are disaggregated at each step. For instance, an all-Union ministry will receive its control targets, which are then disaggregated by branches within the ministry, and so on, until each enterprise under the ministry receives its own control figures. Here the planning branch of the ministry receives its own control figures. Here the planning branch of the ministry prepares a list of tentative input requirements, based on the ministry's control figures, for internal use by each enterprise.

The fourth step relates to the flowing back of the information from the enterprise to the Gosplan. The enterprise will state its input requirements to its immediate superior, who in turn will aggregate the requirements of all the enterprises under him and so on, up to the ministry and then to the Gosplan. At every stage in the process, the proposed inputs are compared with earlier estimated input needs and the correction principle is used to adjust differences between the two.

The fifth step is the crucial step when the plan is finally drawn up. It is followed by submission to and approval by the USSR Supreme Soviet.

Material Balances

The consistencey of control figures is achieved by the Gosplan by drawing up *material balances* of important commodities, labour, finances etc., for the national economy as a whole. The inter-sectoral balance is also acquiring increasing importance. A material balance is said to be achieved when the planned supplies of each commodity equals its targeted material input requirements and final uses.

The labour balances make it possible to distribute manpower resources, proportionately among all the sectors of the economy and help to fix stages for the training of skilled personnel and to establish the required proportions in the use of manpower resources.

The value balances help ensure proper correlation in the distribution of the national product and national incomes between the revenue and expenditures of the population and other value proportions of the national economy.

The balance method of planning is used not only in drafting the general economic plans for the national economy as a whole but also for the Union Republics, particular sectors of the economy, economic areas, territories and regions.

The system of material balances makes it possible to plan the required industrial and inter-sectoral physical proportions in the process of production and distribution. The simplest material balances coordinate different types of production and their component parts within one sector (e.g. iron ore, pig iron and coke balances in the iron-and-steel industry). In more complex material balances, every particular branch is coordinated with all the other economic branches which consume its produce.

Material balances for a number of commodities like coal, cement, electric power, machine tools, etc., are drawn up in physical terms. Along with these, balances of individual types of output like industrial equipment, building materials, etc., are drafted in terms of money.

The material balances are drawn up for the country as a whole and for each of the Union Republics. They are also drawn for fuel, timber, building materials, iron and steel, fertilisers and other industrial items which are consumed in large quantities.

A specimen of a material balance for a particular type of producer goods is given below.

Resources	*Distribution of Resources*
Total	Total
Production	Production and operational needs
Imports	Capital construction
Other receipts	Market stocks
Carryover at the beginning of the plan plan period	Exports
	Other expenditure items (replenishment of reserves, etc.)
	Carryover at the end of the plan period.

For a better understanding of this technique, we give below a hypothetical example of a material balance for steel:

Material Balance for Steel

(in tons)

Resources		*Distribution of Resources*	
Total	2020	Total	2020
Production	2000	Coal industry	200
Imports	20	Steel industry	400
Stocks	0	Machine building	1,000
		Consumer goods industry	300
		Exports	100
		Domestic uses	20

The most pivotal elements in the drafting of a material balance are thorough calculation of the requirements for certain types or groups of products and estimates of available resources.

Requirements for the means of production are determined, as a rule, by the method of simple calculation. For instance, the amount of fuel required by railway transport is calculated on the basis of the volume of freight carriage in gross ton-kilometres and the fixed rates of fuel consumption per 10,000 gross ton-kilometres. Moreover, the need for production reserves, which are strictly regulated, is duly taken into account.

Whenever a gap occurs between requirements and available resources in the process of drafting a material balance, measures are taken to eliminate the discrepancy. In such cases, the planning authorities have five options open to them.

The first option is to order an increase in the planned output of the deficit commodity. This approach would, however, throw the remaining sectors out of balance. For instance, if coal is found to be a deficit commodity and it is decided to balance this by increasing its output, then the balances of other commodities, like steel, electricity, machinery, etc., would have to be revised upwards which in turn would put some other commodities out of balance. For obvious reasons this method of achieving balance is rarely used in the Soviet Union.

The second option is to increase the imports of the deficit commodity. The major snag in this approach is that it would make the consistency of the plan dependent on foreign suppliers and would require use of valuable foreign exchange if imported from the West. Even within the CMEA everything may be jeopardised if the delivery deadlines are not met.

A third option is to direct the enterprise to use substitutes which are not in short supply or by reducing their overall inputs.

A fourth option is to reduce the final demand for the deficit commodity. This could be done by reducing either exports, household demand or investment demand. The positive feature of this approach is that inter-industry balance is not disturbed.

Finally, the planning body may draw upon the stocks of deficit commodity. This method has also been rarely used in the Soviet Union as it is likely to reduce the stock of strategic suppliers.

The most commonly used methods in balancing techniques are the third and the fourth options mentioned above.

Balances in Agricultural Sector

In the agriculture sector the material balances for agricultural produce differ from the balances of industrial items. There are two types of balances of agricultural production: balance of total resources, and balance of the marketable share of resources which goes to the state.

The planning of agricultural production raises problems different from those raised by the planning of industrial production. Agricultural production has to deal with vegetable and animal kingdom; economic activity in this sphere largely depends on natural soil and climatic conditions, notably on soil fertility. The economic process of reproduction is here influenced by the natural process. The seasonal character of agriculture demands that plan targets should be drawn up and organisational measures worked out separately for each individual season.

The special nature of the agricultural sector requires that a definite proportion of its output must be held back for use as means of production. Moreover, the higher the rate at which farm production develops, the bigger is the amount of produce that must remain at the disposal of agricultural enterprises for expanded reproduction. Thus a certain proportion of the total output of grain, potatoes and other crops must be left for seed and fodder, and a certain number of cattle for reproduction and expansion of the main herd. These obligatory deductions from total production require that very careful balance calculations must be made of the volume of farm output at all stages of planning at central and local levels, particularly in the planning of state purchases.

The Soviet Union has steadily developed and improved the system of indicators used by the state in the planning of agricultural production. However, at present indicators are limited to certain decisive aspects of agricultural development.

The most important of these relates to the volume of state purchases of the basic types of produce supplied by crop and livestock farming. This is the chief indicator which is used in the drafting of the agricultural plan, in determining the main proportions and rates of development of farm production. The targets for deliveries to the state are fixed for the Union Republic and include individual targets for collective farms and state farms. The overall plan contains targets regarding the contribution of the Union Republics to the nation-wide fund of specified quantities of meat and meat products, eggs, potatoes, vegetables, melons, fruits and berries, grapes, dried fruit, etc. Targets are also fixed for the delivery of breeder stock in general and of specified breeds of beef and dairy cattle, sheep, goats and pigs.

Farm production is planned by the state farms and collective farms themselves. The volume of state purchases of agricultural produce is the only target set by the state. The planning of crop areas and of livestock farming is carried out by the collective farms and state farms with a view to achieving the required level of production.

Besides making use of these indicators in the planning of agricultural production, use is also made of calculation indicators such as crop areas and yields, the value of gross farm output in comparable and current prices in the Union Republics, utilisation of the arable land and the allotment of land for specific crops, the use of local fertilisers, the head of cattle, the poultry count and the number of hives of bees, balance estimates of fodder, and gross output of grain, oilseeds, potatoes, vegetables, fruits, grapes, meat, milk, eggs, etc.

However, state procurements of agricultural products are by far the most important elements in the planning of agricultural production. They now cover 85 per cent of the total marketable farm produce and about 95 per cent of the total output of grain, meat and milk. Procurement prices, plan targets and others can either stimulate or retard production in agriculture. State procurement also constitutes a link between agriculture and industry.

The planning of state purchases is essential to meet the country's requirements for agricultural produce. In the Soviet Union, it is the state's responsibility to supply the population with food stuffs and industry with raw materials and build up adequate stocks for exports, replenishment of state reserves, etc.

While determining the overall requirement, a clear distinction is made between the requirements of the society as a whole and the need for the building-up of the state reserves. As regards products such as cotton, flax, sugar beet, tobacco, wool, etc., which are entirely sold to the state, the needs of the society and the building up of reserves coincide. In the case of grain, potatoes, vegetables, butter, oil-bearing crops, meat, milk, fat, etc., the volume of purchases is fixed in conformity with the need to build up state reserves which comprise only a part of the society's requirements.

The planning of state procurement begins by estimating the country's requirements for the given product. While estimating such requirements, the planning body is guided by many factors such as growth of population, especially in urban areas, changes in the distribution of national income between the consumption and accumulation funds, wage increases, growth of collective-farmers incomes, price changes, volume of exports, accumulated reserves and changes in population's dietary habits.

The planning of state procurement of such products as grain, potatoes, vegetables, milk, etc., sizeable proportion of which remains with the state or collective farms, is a far more complicated task. It requires balance calculations of the state resources of agricultural products as well as production resources of all the farms producing these products.

The volume of procurement is fixed by estimating the state's requirements for each of these products. Let us take the example of grain. While estimating requirements, the planning body considers that there should be enough of grain to provide (i) the population with bread, flour, groats, macaroni and confectionery, (ii) collective farms engaged in growing cotton flax and other industrial raw materials with grain, (iii) enterprises producing alcohol, beer, starch and concentrated fodder with raw materials, (iv) specialised state farms and horse-drawn transport of industrial enterprises with fodder resources (v) for export trade and (vi) for replenishment of state reserves.

In order to determine the total volume of state purchases, it is necessary to exclude from the total requirements, the

Resources	*Distribution of Resources*
1. Carry over at the beginning of the plan period	1. Supply of total
2. Purchases during the plan period:	(a) Marketable flour
	(b) Marketable grain
(a) under the fixed plan	(c) Marketable cereals
(b) over and above plan	(d) Industrial processing of flour and cereals
3. Grain imports	(e) Industrial processing of grain
	(f) Other uses
	(g) Fodder
	2. Exports
	3. Replenishment of state reserves
	4. Carry over at the end of the plan period
Total.	Total. . . . .

amount of grain carried over at the beginning of the plan period and import deliveries. For instance, if the state's total requirement for grain is 70 million tons, the carry over is five million tons and the imports make up two million tons, the overall procurement must be 63 million tons.

The required volume of grain purchases is estimated on the basis of the balance of state grain resources drawn up according to the following model scheme:

The balance of state grain resources is drawn up in a form for a number of years. This helps to reveal the changes in the pattern of grain distribution and changes in each of the balance items. The balances of individual grain crops are drawn up together with the overall grain balance. The planned volume of procurement can also be determined by the balance of gross resources of grain. The plan balance of gross resources (of grain, for instance) is drawn up on the following basis:

1. *Resources*
   1. Stocks at the beginning of the plan period
   2. Gross output
   3. Other receipts

   Total
2. *Distribution of Resources*

1. Consumption in agricultural production (seed stocks, cattle feed, etc.)
2. Sold and issued to collective farmers as payment for labour; contributed to the fund for war veterans, disabled persons, kindergartens and nurseries, public catering, etc.
3. Bonuses as supplementary remuneration for labour (in kind) to state-farm workers.
4. Stocks at the close of the plan period.
5. Total marketable produce including that meant for sale
   (a) to the state
   (b) to cooperative and other organisations
   (c) in the market

Gross output balances indicate the aggregate volume and use of resources for general state requirements, internal production needs, etc.

Similar balances are drawn up for the land under plough, irrigated land, meat procurement, livestock farming, fodder, agricultural machinery, etc.

The balances method is used almost in every sector of economy, including industry, transport and communications, and capital construction. It is also used for planning of material and technical supplies, of manpower resources, of production costs, profits and prices, of real incomes and retail trade, of the national product, etc. Below we give a few examples, selected at random, of balances as used in production capacity, cash incomes and expenditure, manpower resources, retail trade and national product.

Production Capacity Balance

The production capacity balances play an important role in production planning. This balance reflects the available production capacities, their dynamics and rate of efficiency. It provides the basis for planning the volume of production and capital construction. Below we give a hypothetical production capacity balance for steel industry (in million tons):

1. Capacity of open-heart furnaces and converter shops at the beginning of the plan period	70
2. Planned capacity increase at operating enterprises to be achieved through organisational and technical improvements	2
3. To be put into operation in the plan period by way of new construction and reconstruction of existing enterprises	5
4. Withdrawal of capacity in the plan period	1
5. TOTAL CAPACITY BY THE CLOSE OF THE PLAN PERIOD (1+2+3−4)	76
6. Average annual production capacity including capacity of newly-built and reconstructed enterprises in the plan period	72.5
7. Increase achieved through organisational and technical improvements	2
8. Overall Output in the plan period output obtained from newly-built and reconstructed enterprises	67
9. Utilisation of average annual production capactiy	9.1%
including capacity of newly-built enterprises put into operation	75%

While estimating the increase in production capacity, due account is taken of other factors like construction of enterprises and shops, installation of additional equipment, expansion of subsidiary and ancillary lines of production, modernisation of plant, etc. Production capacity balance calculations begin with estimating the available capacity by means of special computations.

Manpower Resources Balance

The rational use of manpower resources is of utmost importance in national economic planning, for, on this depends the rate of expansion of production and the growth in the people's standard of living.

One of the important tasks of national economic planning is to provide all branches of the economy with adequate manpower resources of the required skills. This is achieved by assessing the manpower requirements of the economy and checking them against the available manpower resources. It is only then that the number of students to be enrolled in educational establishments for specialised training is determined and the most rational distribution of labour resources is planned.

The balance of manpower resources is drawn up on a territorial basis and is based on average annual figures. Its indicators are coordinated with the economic plan indicators for the volume of production, construction and freight turnover and extension of social, cultural and welfare services. A summarised version of the manpower balance is given below.

1. Total labour resources:

    (a) able-bodied population of working age
    (b) working persons of older age and under 16

2. Distribution of labour resources
    (a) total employment:

        Factory and office workers
        collective farmers

    (b) full-time students aged 16 and above
        those engaged in domestic work and individual small farming
3. Distribution of manpower by production spheres and economic sectors

Cash Incomes and Expenditures Balance

This balance, which is drawn up for the period covered by the plan, indicates the volume and sources of the population's cash incomes and the pattern of its monetary expenditures. It also reflects the economic relationship between the state and the population, as well as between individuals and population groups. It enables the planners to establish the required proportions between the cash incomes of the population, retail trade turnover and volume of paid services for the USSR as a whole and for each of the Union Republics. A simplified scheme of this balance is given below.

1. *Cash Incomes*

A. Income accruing to the population from state and co-operative enterprises and institutions

1. Wages
2. Cash incomes from collective farms
3. Receipts from the sale of agricultural produce
4. Pensions and allowance
5. Scholarships
6. Receipts from the financial systems (interest on lottery, loans and savings bank deposits, subsidies for housing construction, etc.)
7. Other cash incomes (bonus not included in the wage fund, etc.)
8. Money received by postal orders and letters of credit (minus the remitted sums)

TOTAL

B. Incomes derived from the sale of commodities and from services rendered to the population

1. Proceeds from the sale of agricultural produce to individual citizens
2. Incomes derived by private citizens from service (repairs, sewing, etc.)
3. Netted from sales

TOTAL

Sum total of incomes (A + B)

Decrease in the amount of cash remaining at the disposal of the population

Balance sheet

II *Expenditures and Savings*

A. Personal expenditure in state and cooperative institutions and Savings

1. Purchase of commodities
2. Payment for services
3. Obligatory payments and voluntary contributions (taxes, dues etc.)
4. Savings, purchase of state loan bonds, increase in savings banks and USSR State Bank deposits
5. Money sent by postal orders and letters of credit (minus the amount of money received)

TOTAL

B. Personal expenditures on the purchase of commodities by the population and on payment for services rendered by private citizens

1. Purchase of agricultural products from private citizens
2. Payment for services rendered by private citizens
3. Payment for items bought from population

TOTAL

Sum total of expenditures (A + B)

Increase in the amount of cash remaining at the disposal of the population

Balance sheet

Balance of the National Product

The balance of the production, consumption and accumulation of the national product is an expression of the process of production distribution and consumption of material values on a nation-wide scale and within the key industries and social sectors for the period covered by the plan. The data in the balance reflects the movement of the national product, first, in the material form (as the aggregate of the means of production and consumer goods), and, second, in value terms (as the amount of social labour invested in the production of the given type of goods). This makes it possible to use the plan balance of the national product for ensuring unity of the national physical structure of the product and its value form in national economic plans. A simplified scheme of this balance is given on page 37

BALANCE OF NATIONAL PRODUCT

Indicators	Resources					Distribution					
	Production			Imports	TOTAL	Losses	Consumption		Accumulation	Exports	TOTAL
	State enterprises	*Collective farms*	*Supplementary individual farming*				*Productive (recoupment of production)*	*Non-productive (needs of the population and state)*			
Aggregate national product,											
Product including sector-wise material production of the aggregate national product											
A (Means of production)											
B (Consumer goods)											

Normally, the balance of the national product is calculated in the actual prices of the given period and in comparable prices. This makes it possible to use actual prices for defining the real value relations in a given period, and comparable prices for expressing the dynamics of the physical volume of the national product. The actual prices obtaining at the time of drafting the five-year plan are used as comparable prices in the plan balance.

The Final Version

After the Gosplan has drawn up the material balance and other balances, the final version of the plan is submitted to the USSR Council of Ministers and to the USSR Supreme Soviet for approval. After it has been approved, the final targets are sent down to individual enterprises and institutions. An enterprise's plan in its final form is called *techpromfinplan* (technical-industrial-financial plan) and establishes the enterprise's output targets as well as input allocations, supply plans, delivery plans, financial flows, wage bills, etc.

Investments

While planning new investments (or planning the setting up of new projects) Soviet planners have to decide between alternative courses which are open to them and all of which yield the same increases in capacity. For instance, while deciding on a power project they have to choose between a thermal-or a hydro-or a nuclear-power station, or while deciding on the construction of a railway line, they have to choose between a steam, a diesel or an electric traction. In each case, higher initial investments are more or less compensated by lower operating costs. Then how do the Soviet planners decide whether they should go in for a hydro-power station or a thermal-power station, or to go in for diesel traction or electric traction.

In the past, various techniques have been used to decide on a particular investment. However, since 1969 Soviet planners have been using the *Standard Methodology for Determining the Economic Effectiveness of Capital Investments* which applies a uniform standard norm to all branches of the economy. Under this methodology, the criterion used to compare alternative investment projects is the *Comparative Economic Effectiveness of Capital Investments*. This measurement requires that investment projects be selected so that

$$C_i + E_n K_i = \text{minimum}$$

where C_i stands for the current expenditures of the ith investment variant K_i stands for the cost of investment project and E_n is the function uniform normative coefficient of effectiveness of capital investments, which is the same for all branches.

The *Standard Methodology* has set this normative coefficient at 12 per cent. This methodology calls for evaluating investment projects on the basis of their full costs (operating costs plus imputed capital costs) with imputed capital costs calculated by using a uniform coefficient for all branches.

In the Table below we demonstrate the working of this technique. Let us assume that Soviet planners are faced with three alternative investment projects. This shows that projects having large investment outlays have low operating costs and vice-versa.

Computation of the "Comparative Economic Effectiveness" of Three Investment Projects

Project	Operating costs (C)	Investment outlays (K)	Uniform normative coefficient (%)	Full costs
	(1)	(2)	(3)	(1 +(3 × 2))
1.	400	500	12	460.0
2.	380	520	12	442.4
3.	370	550	12	436.0

The projects in the example cited above could refer to investment project within a branch or in different branches. Since the normative coefficient is the same for the entire economy, there will be no difference in the evaluation process. The Standard Methodology calls for the selection of projects which have the lowest costs, i.e. the lowest full costs. In the above table, the project with lowest full costs is at No. 3.

Along with this, the Standard Methodology also provides

detailed discounting procedures for evaluating, in present value terms, projects whose operating expenditures and capital outlays change over time. It suggests using a discount rate of eight per cent which is held to be in line with current depreciation procedures.

Finally, the Gosplan has allowed deviations from the normative coefficient for projects to be established in the Far North whose development has been given a high priority. If one were to apply the uniform normative coefficient everywhere, many projects would never come up in the Far North because of various factors.

References

1. V.I. Lenin, collected works, vol. 31, p. 511
2. Lenin, collected works, vol. 27, p. 268
3. Lenin, collected works, vol. 28, p. 36
4. Lenin, collected works, vol. 27, p. 127
5. Lenin, collected works, vol. 30, p. 334
6. Lenin, collected works, vol. 33, p. 166
7. Lenin, collected works, vol. 28, p. 400
8. Lenin, collected works, vol. 27, pp. 207-8
9. Lenin, collected works, vol. 31, p. 511
10. Lenin, collected works, vol. 32, p. 143
11. A. Yesipov, *V. chikh Rukakh Khozyaistov Strany?* Moscow, 1975, p. 3
12. *Ibid,* p. 14
13. R. Chwieduk *et al* Ekonomia Polityczna, Vol. 2, Warsaw, 1966, p. 172, cited in J. Wiczynski, The Economics of Socialism, London, 1970, p. 33
14. B.I. Braginsky, "planning and Management in the Soviet Economy", in The Soviet planned Economy, Moscow, 1974, p. 134
15. *Ibid*

3

THE SYSTEM OF ECONOMIC MANAGEMENT: NEED FOR A CHANGE

In the early years of economic development, the Soviet economy achieved very high rates of economic growth, but over the years, particularly after the Second World war, the growth rates have declined not only in the USSR but also in the Eastern Europe. Incidentally, they have since started picking up again. As we shall see in the succeeding pages, the main reason for this decline was that the Soviet economy had grown much more complex and had entered the *intensive* phase of economic development. This threw up new challenges. The methods and approaches developed in the early phase of economic development were proving an impediment in the further growth of the economy. This called for new approaches and new thinking. This set into motion a process of change in the planning methods and approaches which came to be known as economic reforms. Therefore, the approach refined in the twenty-seventh congress could be related to the earlier reforms. One could say that the new approaches are much bolder and quite imaginative.

The Need for Economic Reforms

The year 1965 marked the beginning of an era of economic reform in the Soviet Union and East European countries. Till 1965, the planning activity had been highly centralised in almost all these countries, and the production decisions were passed down to the industrial enterprises to the minutest detail. Thus one of the important features of the economic reform was to decentralise the process of making economic (production) decisions.

The process of decentralisation involved utilization of market mechanism in a restricted form. As a Polish economist Wlodzimierz Brus put it, "decentralisation meant use of regulated market mechanism in a planned economy."[1] The Hungarian economist Bela Csikos-Nagy observed that decentralisation meant "regulating the activity of the enterprises mainly by economic means". According to him "The extremely rich range of means of economic policy, includes production and distribution policy, price and income policy, as well as budgetary and monetary policy. Since the state prefers to rely on economic means in the regulation of economic processes, it endeavours to make maximum use of the opportunities provided by the indirect levers, and to issue direct instructions only when and where indirect regulation does not prove effective."[2]

However, the degree of decentralisation varied among the socialist countries. Some like Hungary and Czechoslovakia, which either heavily depended upon foreign trade or were industrially quite advanced, went the farthest in the use of indirect economic levers while the Soviet Union drastically reduced the number of planned indicators to be used by enterprises but made very restricted use of market mechanism.

One is liable to raise a pertinent question here: why did the Soviet Union and other East European countries feel a need to resort to the use of indirect economic levers? Was the earlier planning system which passed down a large number of planned indicators not adequate?

It is quite well known that the Soviet Union in its earliest phase of industrialisation enjoyed very high rates of industrial growth. According to official Soviet estimates, industrial production during the First Five-Year Plan (1928-32) grew at the rate of 19.2 per cent per annum; during the Second Plan (1933-37), at the rate of 17.2 per cent; during the Third Plan (1938-40), 15.4 per cent; Fourth Plan (1947-50), 22.7 per cent; Fifth Plan (1951-53), 13.2 per cent. The growth rate of the national income was also higher. The growth rate of net material product in the Soviet Union between 1928-40 was 15 per cent at 1926-27 prices, and between 1950-60, 10 per cent at 1955 prices.

It has been estimated that the average annual growth rate of the Soviet economy between 1928 and 1972 was 5.1 per cent as against 3.2 per cent for the United States for the same period. If we eliminate the war years, the Soviet growth rate rises to 5.5 per cent which is 2.5 per cent higher than the US growth rate.[3]

This indicates that the planning strategy and the approach adopted during the 'thirties, 'forties and, 'fifties had achieved remarkable economic results. Then why economic reforms or use of indirect economic levers? The reason is that because of tremendous growth, the Soviet economy as well as economics of other socialist countries had been undergoing important qualitative and quantitative changes. A particular strategy which achieved tremendous success under different conditions, could not be successfully pursued now. The strategy of the 'forties also brought out its deficiencies clearly in the 'fifties. That is why in the 'fifties economists from the Soviet Union and other East European countries started discussing economic reforms.

It was observed in Czechoslovakia that the annual rate of increase of labour productivity had been going down for a number of years. The year 1962 was the worst, for in that year, the falling labour productivity coupled with acute labour shortage and an over-ambitious investment programme created such an impasse that many investment projects had to be shelved. In the Soviet Union, during the same period, the labour productivity failed to increase as planned. On the contrary, total employment and consequently the total wage bill increased more than what had been planned for. The investment-output ratio instead of decreasing began to increase.

The annual rate of growth in Czechoslovakia for the years 1961-65 dropped to 2 per cent from 7 per cent in the preceding five years; in the GDR, during the same period the growth rate fell from 8 to 3 per cent; in the USSR it fell from 9 to about 6 per cent; in Poland there was a marginal fall from 6.6 to 6 per cent.[4] In Hungary the industrial growth rate during 1962-65 fell to 7.3 per cent from 13.5 per cent in 1960.[5] This was in sharp contrast to annual average growth rate of 13 per cent achieved by all the socialist countries including China, between 1950 and 1959.[6]

The recent figures relating to the growth of national

income for USSR and other East European countries are as follows:

(Average Annual percentage change)

	1951-55	1956-60	1961-65	1966-70	1971-75	1976-80	1980-84
USSR	10.9	9.2	6.5	7.8	5.7	4.3	3.5
Bulgaria	7.8	9.8	6.7	8.7	7.8	6.1	3.9
Czechoslovakia	10.0	7.1	1.9	6.9	5.7	3.7	1.3
GDR	10.0	7.4	4.4	5.2	5.4	4.2	4.3
Hungary	8.5	7.1	4.5	6.8	6.3	3.2	2.1
Poland	11.0	7.0	6.2	6.0	9.8	1.2	1.6
Romania	13.0	7.5	9.1	7.7	11.3	7.3	4.7

Source: Paresh Chattopadhyay, "On Economic Crisis and Transition from capitalism: A Marxian Approach", *Economic and Political Weekly*, 6 Sept. 1986, p. 1582.

It may however be noted that the lower growth rates of the USSR were still higher than the growth rates of the capitalist economies. According to 1983 study of the IMF, "The Soviet economy did not slow as much as the US economy during the world-wide recession, and now the Soviets are moving ahead a little faster."[7] The same report says that the Soviet economy grew by an annual 4 per cent during 1976-80 compared with 3.7 per cent in the US.

Commenting editorially on Reagan's outburst against the socialist economies, the *Times of India* of 15 February, 1984, noted: "The average rate of growth in the Comecon has been consistently higher than that in the OECD through the 'seventies, continuing through the first three years of the 'eighties. There is no indication that this trend is going to be reversed although the average rates for both the OECD and the CMEA have fallen when compared to the past. Between 1971-80, the respective average rates were 3.4 per cent and 5.4 per cent. Between 1980-82, they were 1.2 per cent and 2.9 per cent. Indeed there has not been a single year in the entire post-war period when the average rate of growth of the "developed market economies" has surpassed that of the "centrally planned economies". This fact has also been corroborated by a massive CIA study released in December 1982; this study analysed the growth and development of the Soviet economy over the past three decades.[8]

Nevertheless, the falling growth rates in the USSR compared to their past performance had been a cause of concern. And as the phenomenon was being analyzed, it was becoming clear that the old methods and old approaches to planning were coming in the way of achieving higher growth rates.

Under the pre-1965 system of economic planning, once the plan targets were fixed by the planning authorities through the feedback system, the individual enterprises had to simply carry out the plan directives. All the plan indicators — gross output, assortment of goods, prices, number of persons to be employed, the total wage bill etc., were fixed by the Soviet planning body GOSPLAN. The raw materials and other immediate goods were also centrally allocated to individual enterprises — there was no wholesale trade in intermediate goods, nor could the enterprises determine their sources of raw materials. The funds for new investment as well as for expansion came from budgetary grants. The managers' only job then was to carry out the instructions of the GOSPLAN. It would appear that plans in the earlier phase of Soviet economic development were quite rigid. This is true only to some extent. For, firstly, the planners have been regularly revising the target figures and secondly, the maintenance of inventories of certain important intermediate goods also provided some flexibility to the planners.

However, the wide success of the relatively rigid Soviet plans of the 'thirties and 'forties was due to what economists have come to call the "extensive phase" of Soviet economic development. In the 'thirties the emphasis was on the rapid creation of industrial base and the expansion of industries. The large influx of labour from the villages into towns and new industrial centres led to the increase in the number of industrial units at a very fast pace. At that time quality was not the main concern. As Alec Nove puts it, "such problems as training factory labour, and building great new industrial complexes, seemed much more important than 'efficiency' or replacing machines by better machines."[9]

There had always been a shortage of skilled labour in the

Soviet Union but the unskilled labour had been plentiful. In other words, the emphasis was not on increasing labour productivity but on setting up as many industries as possible. During the First Five-Year Plan, industrial employment almost doubled and at the end of the Second Plan it had increased three times over 1928. During the First Plan, "a total of 23,300 million roubles were invested in industry, whereas the plan provided for only 18,800 million."[10] On 1 April, 1929 there were 1.47 million persons on the register of labour exchange in the USSR but by October 1932, there was not one registered as unemployed.[11]

But this situation had radically changed by the 'fifties. Huge manpower losses during the Second World War and relative drying up of labour supply from the countryside now created shortage of unskilled labour. The implication of this new development was quite clear — increased production could now come only from increased labour productivity. This, in turn, called for constant development of new technologies and techniques of production and periodic replacement of existing plants and equipments. In other words, the Soviet Union in the 'fifties had entered a period of 'intensive' economic growth (in contrast to the extensive phase of the 'thirties and the 'forties) and the key to higher economic growth rates lay in increasing labour productivity.

The successive Soviet plans after the war had stipulated that more than 75 per cent of the increase in output was to come from increased labour productivity and the rest from increased employment. But the final results invariably revealed that while labour productivity lagged behind than what had been planned for, the actual wage fund exceeded the planned one. For instance, between 1956 and 1960, total employment grew by over 10 million compared to planned 5 million. Again, between 1959 and 1965, labour productivity increased by 42 per cent compared to the planned target of 45 to 50 per cent; number of workers and employees rose by 37 per cent against planned 22 per cent and the total wage fund by 68 per cent as against planned 54 per cent.[12] This led the 23rd Congress of the CPSU to observe that the rate of growth of production and productivity had somewhat slowed down in the last years of the seven-year plan (1959-1965), the efficiency of production assets and the effectiveness of capital investments had dropped and that there were delays in starting new enterprises. As Maurice Dobb observes: "Thus there was accumulating evidence of an important problem: that the traditional system was more successful apparently, in achieving increases in quantity of output than it was in raising productivity per man by means of constant technical innovation . . . . a problem likely to become progressively more important as reserves of new labour were exhausted and shortages of manpower became a crucial bottleneck."[13]

A second reason why the traditional planning methods succeeded in attaining high growth rates was the cushion provided by the consumers goods sector. During the pre-war planning years, the emphasis was on the quick development of the priority sector. The priority sector was defined to include heavy industry only—fuel and power, machine building, basic metals and so on. Thus by definition, the consumers goods fell in the non-priority sector and were therefore made to bear the brunt of economic development. Whenever the shortages developed or the units failed to fully meet the supplies of scarce inputs to the priority sectors, the allocations of such inputs made to the consumers goods sector were diverted to meet the requirements of the priority sector. The consumers goods sector was asked to do with second best and even third best substitutes. Sometimes they were asked to do without the raw materials and were thus allowed to fall short.

A third factor for the wide success of the traditional planning method was that there were fewer number of industrial units, fewer number of inputs and fewer number of final goods to administer. In the early 'thirties the balance method of planning and allocation of various kinds of inputs covered a few hundred items. It was then relatively easy to make the necessary adjustments if there were bottlenecks. By 1950, this number had grown to about 2,000 and by 1965 GOSPLAN was handling 10,000 products for central allocation. Thus the problem of adjustment through balance methods became more complex. For instance, a shortfall in the production of steel necessitate corresponding changes in all the industries using steel and machinery as input and all other industries using steel and machinery for their final products. Over-production does not create much of a problem. But a shortfall in actual production of a particular commodity necessitates revision of many material balances. Now with a large number of items covered by the material balances adjustment has become a time-consuming process. Recent census of Soviet industry reveals that there are more than 50,000 different industrial enterprises in the USSR. It is true that the GOSPLAN deals with a limited number of commodities, even then the number was very large on the eve of the economic reform. It draws up more than 2,000 material balances.[14] Industrial supply and distribution plan compiled by GOSPLAN have been known to total 70 volumes of almost 12,000 pages and deal with well over 30,000 commodities.[15]

In the course of the implementation of the traditional planning strategy, it was observed that many unhealthy practices had crept in which were reflected in the falling growth rates.

The strategy of providing interest-free investment funds through budgetary grants led to many undesirable tendencies. One of the tendencies noted among the enterprises, was to overstate their requirements and understate their potentialities and thus hold spare capacity of their plant and equipment beyond their normal needs. This had become a regular practice with many managers. But in terms of cost to the economy, the scarce resources were tied up in spare capacity.

The planning of the 'thirties and early 'fifties also led to excessive bureaucratisation of the planning system. It is reported that in 1969, the industrial supply network alone employed about half a million people. In the same context one of the Soviet newspapers noted that "requisition for ball bearings by one auto-factory alone was processed in all by fourteen agencies and some 430 pounds of documents were generated."[16] Another instance of bureaucratic red tapism is provided by 91 volumes of engineering data generated in the planning of a new steel mill.[17] It would not be far-fetched to say that excessive bureaucratic work often led to delays in the commissioning of projects.

The index of 'gross output' as the basic success indicator

of an enterprise also led to waste. The manager of an undertaking became more interested in fulfilling the output plan rather than in improving the quality of the product. This was rather plainly pointed out in a report to the Central Committee of the CPSU: "As seen from experience, the index of overall volume of output does not stimulate the enterprise to produce goods which are really needed by the national economy and the public, and in many cases tends to limit any improvement in the assortment of goods produced and their quality. Not infrequently our enterprises are producing low quality goods which the consumer does not want and which therefore remain unsold."[18]

Many a time, the index of gross output was in terms of weight, as so many tons of agricultural machinery or so many tons of nails and so on. This gave rise to the unhealthy practice of producing heavier goods. Once the Russian satirical magazine *Krokodil* carried a cartoon depicting workers in procession carrying aloft one gigantic nail, and the caption read "The Factory Fulfils its Plan". A few economists in the Soviet Union have estimated the waste of steel involved in the fulfilling of weight plan. Professor A. Tselikov says: "Analysis shows that 18 to 25 per cent more metal is being used per unit of engineering in our country than in some other countries . . . in excessive weight of machines we are losing 9-12 million tons of metal a year."[19] Similarly when the index of cloth production was expressed in terms of so many million metres of cloth, the mills found it easier to meet the plan target by producing narrow cloth of simplest weave.

Another factor which forced the industrial units to adopt unhealthy industrial practices was the sharp contradiction between the wide time horizon of the Central plan and very narrow horizon of the enterprises. In an effort to meet their plan targets fixed by the GOSPLAN, the enterprises often used less economic methods. But such diversionary techniques helped the enterprises to achieve results within the plan period.[20]

This over-emphasis on meeting the gross output target however, precluded many industrial undertakings from adopting new processes and new equipment. Since the introduction of new technology entailed some loss of production during the installation period many managers would not take the risk, for fear that they may not achieve the plan target. The Soviet newspaper *Pravda* once related in 1958 a story of an inventor of an efficient small boiler. He could not find any enterprise to take up its production on commercial basis because the output plans for boilers were expressed in terms of area of heating surface. In other words antipathy towards new products and processes was in-built in the planning strategy which emphasised excessive central control.

In the late 'fifties a situation had been reached where every move of an enterprise was planned by the GOSPLAN. There were instances where an enterprise was given 500 targets and indices to be fulfilled. As a consequence, an enterprise was left with hardly any chance "of significantly influencing the content of their own plan."[21]

By planning everything in such minute details, the GOSPLAN had cluttered itself with so many decision-making processes that it was sure to create "planned bottlenecks".

The quantitative and qualitative changes taking place in the Soviet economy since the 'thirties were making it difficult for the economy to grow within the traditional planning framework. Even though the growth rates in the Soviet economy after the 'fifties had been much higher than what they were in the capitalist countries, the fact that they were much below the domestic rates of the 'thirties had prompted the Soviet government to reassess its traditional planning approach.

The Party and the Government could not now ignore the rising expectations of the people. In the late 'fifties increasing attention towards the consumers goods industries meant that this sector could no longer be used as a cushion for the priority sector. As the planners started talking about 'balanced production programme' and 'optimal planning', the distinction between priority and non-priority sectors became redundant. And this necessitated that consumers goods sector produces ony those goods which are in demand, since as Dobb says ". . . the retail market is a market in the full sense under socialism, it follows that production in Dept. 2 (consumers goods sector) must always be more concerned with the market and with the peculiarities of individual demand than in Dept. 1 (producers goods sector)."[22]

By the early 'sixties it was becoming clear that the extensive phase of development was coming to a close and that the economy could grow at the rate of the 'thirties, provided the labour productivity increased at a fast rate. This was possible only if new technologies were developed rapidly and adapted speedily by the industrial units.

Thus it was in resposne to the quantitative and qualitative changes taking place in the Soviet economy, and the shortcomings of the traditional planning methods, that the discussion on economic reforms was initiated in the early 'sixties. The first attempts to initiate economic reforms were made in the mid 'fifties, but they were half-hearted and mostly took the form of administrative reshuffle.

In 1957, there was an attempt to reorganise the planning system on regional basis. By this measure, it was sought to break up the all-powerful ministries which over the years had grown into powerful bureaucratic empires. By appointing regional economic councils (*Sovnarkhozy*) an attempt was made to take adminstration closer to production but there was no autonomy for undertakings. On the contrary, this made matters worse by creating vested regional interests. Sovnarkhozy encouraged regional loyalty in the allocation of necessary inputs and outputs. Anyway this attempt failed to check the falling growth rates.

It was the comprehensive report of the Soviet Government on the functioning of the enterprises and on proposed economic reforms which brought about many important changes in the implementation of the planning strategy. As one Polish economist pointed out, these reforms were not an end in itself but were "designed to increase the effectiveness of economic outlays . . . ."

The proposals for the renewed discussion on economic reforms were first put forward by E.G. Liberman in an article published in the *Pravda*. The editor's note to the article read: "The materials published in *Pravda* on questions of perfecting economic management and planning, are arousing great interest on the part of the public. Important and basic questions are raised in today's article. The editors of *Pravda* attaching greater significance to these questions, invite economics scholars and officials of industry and of planning and economic agencies to express their opinions regarding the author's specific proposals." (*Pravda*, 19 September, 1962).

The essence of Liberman's proposal was that there should be no "petty tutelage" of industrial managements and that in day-to-day implementation of production policy "administrative methods" be replaced by more "indirect economic instruments" of control such as prices, taxes, rental charges, interest charges and so on; that the enterprises should function on *Khozraschyot* (commercial accounting) basis and show balance sheet profits (or losses); and that rewards be given on the basis of profits.

It will, however, be wrong to conclude that the Soviet economists were advocating free market economy. On the contrary it was clearly pointed out that central planning of output would be maintained in full vigour and that rewards for profits would be given only if the important output targets for quantity and assortment had been met. Those enterprises which failed to meet the output targets would be deprived of any right to bonuses. Thus it was never proposed that profits act as fundamental guide to economic activity, but it was felt that profits would have a little more important role to play along with other success criteria. It was thought that profits along with bonuses and reduced number of Central directives would encourage managers to seek out economies in cost and find out new reserves rather than build up excess stocks.

The proposals were followed by intense discussions for about three years. There were some who opposed the proposed economic reforms; there were others who supported the proposals and there were still others, particularly those belonging to the mathematical school, who wanted to go many steps further than the proposed reforms.

Economic reforms were introduced on an experimental basis in the consumers goods sector especially in the clothing and footwear industry. Commenting upon the success of the experiments, the Chairman of the Council of Ministers of the USSR pointed out in his report: "The new system of planning and economic stimulation increased the workers' interest in the results of their work. In the course of four months of work under the new conditions (May-August, 1965) empty runs were reduced by 15 per cent, and the freight turnover jumped by 34 per cent as a result. Labour productivity went up by 31 per cent and profits more than doubled, making it possible to raise the workers' wages. The profits for the five organizations, over and above the planned level totalled 969,000 roubles in four months. As before, they transferred 40 per cent of profits to the state budget, and the balance — over 550,000 roubles — was used for improving the production base, accumulating reserves, for socio-cultural requirements and for the material stimulation of the workers." But it was in September 1965 that the Soviet Premier announced a set of economic reforms. They are known as the Soviet Government Reforms of 1965.

The main thrust of the reforms was reduction in the number of enterprise targets from above and replacement of gross output by sales as the prime indicator of success of an enterprise. Similarly reforms introduced one labour indicator — the quantum of wage fund — compared to four earlier. An enterprise manager was now handed down eight targets or indicators compared to twenty to thirty in the pre-1965 period. The eight targets given to an enterprise were as follows:

1. The volume (and value) of goods to be sold.
2. The main assortments of goods.
3. Its rate of profits and the level of cost accounting (profitability).
4. Its wages fund.
5. Its payments into the state budget and allocations from the state budget.
6. The volume of centralised capital investments and the putting into operation of production capacities and fixed assets.
7. The main assignments for introducing new technology.
8. The indices of material and technical supplies.

As the Soviet Premier pointed out, "All other indices of

economic activity will be planned by the enterprise independently, without endorsement from a higher organization. This will relieve the enterprises from excessive control and will permit them to adopt the most economic decisions in the light of actual conditions of productions."[23]

A second important feature of the reforms was that in matters of financing the enterprise investment, the importance of state budget was reduced and that of the Gosbank (Central Bank of the USSR) was increased. The Gosbank now provided investment funds at differential rates of interest. It also now handled the task of clearing debts among enterprises and also between enterprises and their customers in the trade network. The main idea behind this move was to reduce the role of budgetary grants as a source of investment finance as also to reduce the role of subsidy. It also sought to establish production development fund which was to be made of profits, depreciation and the sales of unneeded equipment. An important major departure from the previous practice was that the profitability of an enterprise was now calculated in relation to capital rather than cost.

Along with managerial reforms, industrial prices were also revised upward to allow many enterprises to be profitable under normal circumstances. A number of enterprises had been suffering losses because of the average branch cost pricing. Until 1967, the profit mark-up was planned at 5 to 10 per cent of the branch average cost of production. The main purpose of fixing new prices was to enable most enterprises to cover their cost of production, earn enough profit to pay a 6 per cent charge on capital, establish incentive funds and expand their capital. Thus the industrial prices after 1967 were fixed in such a way that they ensured normal profit of 12-15 per cent on fixed and working capital and fully covered the average branch cost of production.

Though profits have always been a part of the Soviet managerial system, it was now given a prominent position along with other indicators. Profit now has been made an important source for decentralised investment by the enterprise manager. Besides, the enterprise also operates material incentive funds which now come out of profits; earlier incentives were paid out of wage fund. The material incentive fund is subdivided into three funds[24]. The first fund is meant for giving incentives to the workers; individual workers or a group of workers are paid from it, for some outstanding performance. The second fund is for social and cultural purpose. It is used to improve social and medical services for the staff of an enterprise, pay for medicines and equipment required by medical establishments, provide accommdation at holiday centres and sanatoria, better meals for children at kindergarten, factory conveyance for outings and so on. The third is a housing fund which is used to construct and repair houses, clubs, holiday centres, canteens, etc.

Four years after the introduction of economic reforms, a new formula was devised to test the comparative economic effectiveness of capital investments. Under the earlier formula, the annual operating cost difference between two variants was compared to the capital cost of difference, through the following ratio, called the coefficient of relative effectiveness.

$$CRE = \frac{(C_2 - C_1)}{(I_1 - I_2)}$$

Where I refers to initial capital outlays (of the projects 1 and 2) and C represents annual operating expenses of projects 1 and 2

Its reciprocal $1/E = T$ gave the recoupment period and denoted the number of years necessary for the investment to be recovered.

The new 1969 formula known as the Standard Methodology for Determining the Economic Effectiveness of Capital Investments is as follows:

$$C_i + E_n K_i = \text{minimum}$$

Where C_i stands for the current expenditures of i th investment variant

K_i stands for the cost of investment project, and E_n is the normative coefficient of effectiveness of capital investments.

The Standard Methodology (as discussed in the preceding chapter) has set this normative coefficient at 12 per cent. This methodology calls for evaluating investment projects on the basis of their full costs (operating costs plus imputed capital costs) with imputed capital costs cacluated by using a uniform coefficient for all branches.

Coming to the question of managerial economic reforms, about 83 per cent of the enterprises had been converted to the *Khozraschyot* system by 1970. This covered 93 per cent of the total output, 95 per cent of the total industrial profits and 92 per cent of the total industrial workers.

The new economic reforms were also not without their shortcomings as the authorities realised in the course of implementation of these reforms.

These related to unduly large share of bonus funds received by managerial personnel, lack of attention to labour productivity and quality of products, the unwillingness of managers to economise costs etc. Thus between 1971 and 1973 the economic reforms were further revised.

The more flexible system of enterprise incentive fund was replaced by a somewhat rigid one; the ministry within the limits laid down by the GOSPLAN, now determined the size of enterprise incentive funds by fixing the planned incentive fund target. Thus the actual size of various incentive funds was now dependent upon the fulfilment of output, profitability and labour productivity targets, fulfilment of plan for key products in physical units, plan for consumers goods and plan for changes in product quality and new products.

Strict controls were also placed over the distribution of incentive funds. Limits were placed on the rate of growth of managerial bonuses; average wages were not to increase at a rate faster than the rate of growth of labour productivity and bonuses differentials among different branches were also regulated. Bonuses paid to the managerial cadre were now tied to fulfilment of sales and profitability plans and the fulfilment of the physical assortment plan.

The managers' control over the size of production development fund was also curtailed and six more indices were added to the centrally planned targets. These related to labour productivity, gross output, material and fuel economy, quality targets and consumers goods targets.

The initial impact of the economic reforms on the industrial enterprises was good. Many industrial units recorded increases in profits and sales turnover after adopting economic reforms. For instance, the USSR Ministry of Instrument-Building, Means of Automation, and Central Systems recorded 3.9 per cent increase in sales and 4.8 per cent in profits over the initially established plan. Economic incentive funds rose to 72.5 million. This may not be an impressive gain but, as the minister concerned pointed out, had the enterprises not been converted to the new system, they would have received only 23.8 million roubles, ie ⅓rd of the amount that they actually received. He further observed that even if the initial plans were overfulfilled the enterprises would have received only 41.4 million roubles or a mere 57 per cent of the sum that was left at their disposal after their conversion to the new system.

Let us take another example. The production development fund of an industrial enterprise in Kharkov enabled it to increase its labour productivity. At "shop No. 5", labour productivity increased by 20-25 per cent and this, in turn, enabled the foundry shop to raise labour productivity by 10 per cent. In the space of three years, the average annual increase in the production of central air conditioners was 21 per cent, balance sheet profit increased by 18.3 per cent, production profitability by 14 per cent, and profit per rouble of fixed capital by 15.9 per cent. It is noteworthy that the entire increase in the volume of production was realised exclusively through higher labour productivity without an increase in the number of personnel.

Similarly, there has been considerable saving in the use of fuel resources. For instance in 1978, 70 million tons of conventional fuel was saved when compared with its consumption in 1975. This is the result of introduction of new technology and new techniques. Soviet economists have calculated that if one million tons of rolled steel is not machined, but shaped by more advanced pressure techniques, metal savings will work out at 250,000 tons. This will release 15,000 metal-cutting machines and 20,000 workers. Between 1975 and 1978, the introduction of new technologies in the consumers goods industry, besides improving the quality of such goods, freed 1.3 million workers who were absorbed in fast developing industries.

However, it would be wrong to conclude that reforms were an unqualified success. During its implementation many problems cropped up. For instance, as Ye. Liberman has recorded, at many enterprises which switched over to the new system, production was planned for them in terms of 15 indices instead of 8. This was particularly true of the knit-wear industry. Similarly in an agricultural machine plant, wage fund was still planned on an old basis (based on output per worker and gross output) but since 80 per cent of the staff was employed in the design office, its wage fund was slashed by 190-200 thousand roubles.

In another case, it was found that the Ministry of Ferrous Metallurgy decided to confirm even repair schedules for all open hearth furnaces, rolling mills and all metalurgical equipment. Reacting sharply to this, the Chief economist of the "Red October" Metallurgical plant noted that "for some reasons, they take care of us as if we were little children. If we spend 1,000 roubles on capital repair, we have to write a certificate. We write reports on the work of each unit, with respect to every index. And the number of planning indices is already approaching 20."

This is enough to give an idea of the problems faced in the implementation of economic reforms. But these teething troubles were natural. As the then Chairman of the GOS-PLAN, N.K. Baibakov rightly observed: "....the introduction of the new system requires a change in the methods of production management and necessitates learning how to work under the new system. And this does not come immediately." Many of the shortcomings are also due to the habits of individual personnel. "These shortcomings cannot be eliminated all at once, by an order. The more complete and consistent introduction will result in disappearance of voluntaristic administration."

Some of the shortcomings of the 1965 reform are being overcome through merger of enterprises into what are called "Associations". The decision on mergers was announced in 1973 and became operative by the end of 1975. Under this scheme a number of similar enterprises are combined to form an Association and there will be a single management for them. The major decision-making powers are vested in socialist corporations (Associations), the new middle level of management between the ministry and the enterprise. The powers which were given to the enterprises under 1965 reform now belong to the Associations. The main idea behind mergers is that Associations are better qualified to make planning and resource allocation decisions at the enterprise level than Central planners and ministries, because they are closer to the source of information on which these decisions are based. Almost all the Associations will combine factories, research and design development organizations. However, very little information is available on this aspect to pass any judgement in the matter.

As regards the impact of these reforms on the growth rates (particularly industrial) the available data shows that the reforms have not enabled the Soviet Union to 'recapture' the growth rates of the 'thirties and 'forties but they have definitely checked the slide-back. On the eve of the economic reforms, the industrial growth rate had slid down to around 6 per cent while during the Ninth Plan the industrial growth rate was 7.4 per cent. It must be emphasized here that one per cent in the 'eighties is much 'weighted' or 'loaded' in absolute value than what it was in the 'forties and the 'fifties. Since the extensive phase of development is over, it is unlikely that the industrial growth rates of 'forties and 'fifties can be recaptured. By international standards however, the current Soviet industrial growth rate is much higher — 7.4 per cent as compared to 1.2 per cent in the United States and the EEC countries. The most remarkable thing about the Soviet economy is that despite fall in relative growth rate, it has remained crisis-free. In the capitalist countries, fall in growth rates in recent times has meant recession and unemployment, and fall in the standard of living of the people. The Soviet Union, on the other hand, despite relative fall in growth rates, has remained free from economic crises that overtook the capitalist countries. The stable price level and steadily rising incomes in the Soviet Union stand testimony to this.

This is also admitted by American scholars who have been

giving testimonies before the Congressional Committees. A senior official of the US Central Intelligence Agency said in declassified testimony that a collapse of the Soviet economy is not "even a remote possibility".

"One of the worst things we can do is to underestimate the economic strength of our principal adversary," so observed Senator William Proximire, an opposition democrat from Wisconsin. This was revealed by Mr. Rowen, Chairman of CIA's national intelligence council in December 1982.[25]

There has since been a new approach to economic strategy which can be considered as further refinement of the measures adopted in the early, seventies.

References

1. Wlodzimierz Brus, *The Economics and Politics of Socialism: Collected Essays,* London, Routledge & Kegan Paul, 1973, p. 31.
2. Bela Csikos-Nagy, "Ten Years of Hungarian Economic Reform", *The New Hungarian Quarterly,* Vol. XIX, No. 70, Summer 1978, p. 31.
3. Paul R. Gregory and Robert C. Stuart, *Soviet Economic Performance and Structure,* New York, Harper & Row, 1974, p. 379
4. Wlodzimiers Brus, pp. 33-4.
5. Maurice Dobb, *Socialist Planning: Some Problems,* London, Lawrence & Wishart, 1970, p. 42.
6. United Nations, *World Economic Survey,* 1961.
7. *Times of India,* 5 July 1983.
8. *Patriot,* 26 December 1982 and 11 January 1983.
9. Alec Nove, "Economic Reforms in the USSR and Hungary: A Study in Contrast", in Alec Nove and D.M. Nuti (eds.), *Socialist Economics,* Middlesex, Penguin Books, 1972, p. 336.
10. Vinod Mehta, *Soviet Economic Development and Structure,* New Delhi, Sterling Publishers, 1978, p. 114.
11. *Ibid*, p. 115.
12. Maurice Dobb, pp. 29-30.
13. Maurice Dobb, p. 30.
14. Michael Ellman, "The Consistency of Soviet Plans," in Morris Bornstein and Daniel Fusfeld (eds), *The Soviet Economy,* 4th ed., Illinois, Richard D. Irwin, 1974, p. 67.
15. Paul R. Gregory and Robert C. Stuart, p. 125.
16. *Ekonomicheskaya Gazeta,* 30 March, 1963.
17. Leon Smolnski, "What Next in Soviet Planning", *Foreign affairs,* July 1964, pp. 604.
18. Report to the CPSU Central Committee, 25 Sept. 1968.
19. *Pravda*, 13 September, 1968.

20. Wlodzimierz Brus, p. 39.
21. *Voprosi Ekonomiki* No. 27, 1965, p. 3.
22. Maurice Dobb, p. 31.
23. Report to the CPSU Central Committee, 25 Sept. 1968.
24. Vinod Mehta, *Soviet Economic Policy: Income Differentials in USSR*, New Delhi, Radiant Publishers, 1977, pp. 17 to 21.
25. *Patriot*, 11.1.1983.

4

ELEVENTH AND THE TWELFTH PLANS

The twenty-sixth Congress of the CPSU had stated that its main purpose of the economic and social development during 1981-85 and the period ending in 1990, would be the establishment of the material and technical basis of communism.

The emphasis in the Eleventh Five Year Plan was on improving the administration and management of enterprises and the structure of social production and thereby ensuring the steady growth of the economy and promoting the well-being of the people. But as Prime Minister Nikolai Ryzhkov, in his report to the 27th Congress on the results of the Eleventh Five Year Plan, observed, some of the important tasks could not be accomplished and the results in certain individual years were below the target.

For instance, the Guidelines for the Eleventh Plan had stated that the national income would go up by 18-20 per cent during 1981-85 and by 40 per cent by the year 1990. As for the development of industry, the guidelines had stated that the industrial output in the five years would go up by 26-28 per cent and the labour productivity in industry by 23 to 25 per cent. However, as Ryzhkov pointed out in his report to the 27th Congress, the national income during 1981-85 grew by 17 per cent and industrial output by 20 per cent only. In fact in 1982 the growth of industrial output was 1.5 times below the average of the 10th Five Year Plan. In this connection he noted that "the unfavourable tendencies that had appeared in the economic development in the 1970s grew sharper in the early 1980s rather than slackened. And this had an adverse effect on the fulfilment of the 11th Five Year Plan. The slowdown of the growth rates continued during the first two years." [*Guidelines for the Economic and Social Development of the USSR for 1986-1990 and for the Period Ending in 2000,* Moscow, 1986, p. 8]

A number of factors were responsible for this slowdown. In the words of Prime Minister Ryzhkov: "As for the fundamental causes of the shortcomings, they consist in the following: in practical work timely account was not taken of the changed economic situation mainly due to the exhaustion of the potentialities for extensive growth, and no proper perseverance was displayed in using the achievements of scientific and technological progress, and in restructuring the economy and its management system in accordance with the imperatives of the day. Besides, both in the centre and in the localities, many leaders continued to apply outdated methods and proved unprepared for work in the new conditions. Discipline and order deteriorated impermissibly. There was a lowering of exactingness and responsibility. The vicious practice of the downward revision of plans became widespread."

After this critical assessment, certain steps were taken to tone up the management of the economy and to improve the organisation at the plant level. As a result of these measures initiated in 1983, positive changes were noticeable, and this somewhat improved the situation with the fulfilment of the 11th Five Year Plan. Had the economy not picked up after 1982, the growth rates would have been still lower. As already stated the national income during the 11th Plan grew by 17 per cent as against the target figure of 20 per cent. The actual achievements and the target figures are given on Page 64.

As Mr. Ryzhkov pointed out many industries were not able to reach the planned targets. For the planned period as a whole there was an output shortfall of 35 million tons of finished rolled stock, 145 million tons of coal, over 50 million tons of oil, and consumer goods worth 16 billion roubles. Moreover, the design technical level, and quality of machines and equipment did not meet the requirements of the national economy in all cases. There was a systematic lag in the chemical and the timber and woodworking industries. And as Mr. Ryzhkov noted, "the principal general ministries failed to cope with their plans year after year."

As for the living standards of people there were positive

developments as can be seen from the following table:

	Total for 1981-1985 (in billion roubles)	Absolute growth for 1981-1985 as against 1976-1980 (in billion roubles)	Growth of total volume in 1981-1985 as against 1976-1980, (per cent)	Targets for 1981-1985 as against 1976-1980, (per cent)
National income, share used for consumption and accumulation	2,398	353	117	120
Industrial output	3,778	628	120	126-128
Agricultural output (at 1983 prices)	1,010	53	106	—
Freight turnover of all modes of transport (trillion ton-kilometres)	37.1	5.7	118	118-121
Installed basic assets	815	147	122	—
Capital investment	842	125	117	112-115
Retail trade turnover	1,466	226	118	122-125

Sources: *Guidelines for the Economic and Social Development of the USSR for 1986-1990 and for the period ending in 2000,* Moscow, APN, 1986, pp. 9-10
XXVI CPSU Congress: Documents and Resolutions, Soviet Land Booklets, New Delhi, 1981.

There was a rise in the average monthly pay of factory and office workers and the remuneration of collective farmers. There was an improvement in pension schemes, in the system of health care, and a marked growth of state aid to families with children. Considerable funds were allocated for reform in education and school systems. As in the previous plans, housing construction proceeded on a large scale; as is

	Guidelines targets approved by the 26th Congress	Actual fulfilment
Average monthly wages of factory and office workers, 1985 (in per cent of 1980)	113-116	113
Average monthly payment for the work of collective farmers, 1985 (in per cent of 1980)	120-122	129
Social consumption funds, 1985 (in per cent of 1980)	120	125
Housing completed in 1981-1985, (million square metres overall)	530-540	552
Pre-school facilities completed in 1981-1985 (million places)	2.5	2.9
Completed general schools in 1981-1985, (million places)	4.3	5.2
Hospital beds, 1985 (in per cent of 1980)	108-110	108.7
Specialists trained by institutions of higher learning and specialised secondary schools in 1981-85 (in millions)	10	10.5

Sources: Guidelines for the Economic and Social Development of the USSR for 1986-1990 and for the period ending in 2000, pp. 10, 11

evident from the above table, the built area completed was 552 million square metres against the target of 530-540 million square metres. During the Eleventh Plan, over 10 million flats were constructed and handed over to the families all over the Soviet Union.

Perspective Plan: Upto Year 2000

The guidelines proposed at the 27th Congress of the CPSU for the Twelfth Five Year Plan form part of the wider 15-year perspective plan. The idea is to radically transform the technological base of the country and to profoundly transform its productive forces. These envisaged profound changes cannot be carried out in one or even two plan periods. Therefore 15-year period is considered as the optimal period during which the current major breakthrough in science and technology could be fully achieved.

In the perspective plan the rate of growth remains central to the economic policy. It is envisaged that the national income will grow from an annual average of 3.1 per cent during the Eleventh Plan period to 5 per cent during the Fourteenth Plan period. The emphasis is on checking the fall in growth rates which have been observed in the past. In absolute terms it is envisaged to produce national income (at constant prices) worth about 12 trillion roubles, which will be roughly equal to the total income for all the preceding years of Soviet power.

The increase in growth rate would be achieved through the intensive use of existing machinery and equipment, modernisation of equipment, adoption of new technologies and by raising the productivity of labour. It is proposed to increase the labour productivity in the whole of the Soviet Union 2.3 to 2.5 fold by the year 2000. Moreover, during the whole of the perspective plan period, the emphasis would be on economy in the use of fuel, energy, raw materials, metals and other materials.

At the same time, the living standards of the people would be further improved and quality products would be made available to them. To quote: "In the first place, this means meeting in full the growing effective demand for high quality and diverse goods and services and reaching the rational norms of food intake recommended by science. A task of great social significance is that of providing practically every Soviet family with a separate house-flat or a cottage and has to be carried out by the year 2000.

"The system of education, personnel training and medical services are to be improved radically, and the material facilities for culture, recreation and sport for the entire social sphere, are to be expanded considerably."

The Twelfth Five Year Plan: 1986-1990

As stated earlier, the Twelfth Five Year Plan forms the first stage of the 15-year perspective plan and the aim is to take the economy during the Twelfth Plan "to a higher trajectory of development, the trajectory of acceleration." The main task of the Twelfth Plan is to enhance the growth rate and efficiency of economic development through accelerated scientific and technological progress, the retooling and technical reconstruction of industry, the intensive utilisation of the existing production potential, an improvement of the economic management system and of the economic mechanism.

The Twelfth Five Year Plan aims at steadily raising the growth rates of the various sectors of the economy. The growth rates as given in the table below are quite moderate and quite realistic. The annual growth rate of national income will increase from the present 3.1 per cent to about 3.5 to 4 per cent. The industrial output will grow at an annual rate of 3.9 to 4.4 per cent as against 3.7 per cent during the Eleventh Plan. However, within the industrial sector, the consumers goods sector will grow faster than the capital

Annual Growth Rate Targets for Some Important Sectors of the Economy

	Increment rate in absolute terms (in billion roubles)		Mean annual growth rate (per cent)	
	1985 over 1980	1990 over 1985, under the draft Guidelines	11th Five-Year Plan	12th Five-Year Plan under the draft Guidelines
National income share used for consumption and accumulation	71	96-111	3.1	3.5-4.0
Industrial output of which	135	169-194	3.7	3.9-4.4
means of production (group A)	99	123-142	3.6	3.7-4.2
consumer goods (group B)	36	46-52	3.9	4.1-4.6
Agricultural output (mean annual output growth over the previous Five-Year Plan, in prices at 1983 level	11	28-32	1.1	2.7-3.0
Retail trade turnover	46	59-73	3.1	3.4-4.0
Volume of paid services to the population	9.8	13.7-18.2	5.0	5.4-7.0

Source: *Guidelines for the Economic and Social Development of the USSR for 1986-1990 and for the period ending in 2000* goods sector. The volume of retail trade turnover is also to grow relatively slowly. However, it is in the agricultural sector that the growth rate will be more than doubled i.e., from 1.1 per cent in the preceding plan to about 2.7 to 3.0 per cent during the Twelfth Plan.

During the Twelfth Plan, the emphasis would be on increasing the productivity through intensive use of existing investment. As stated in the Guidelines: "The growth of end results will take place in conditions of substantial reductions in increments of the basic resources and simultaneous improvements in the qualitative indicators of work." The envisaged increment rates are given in the Table below:

	Increment for five years (per cent)		Growth (+), fall (−) of increment rates
	1981-1985	1986-1990 under the draft Guidelines	
I. *Results of Production*			
National income share used for consumption and accumulation	17	19-22	+2—+5
Industrial output	20	21-24	+1—+4
Agricultural output (mean annual volume)	6	14-16	+8—+10
II. *Key Resources*			
Number of people employed in material production	2.3	0.5	−1.8
Fixed production assets	37	30	−7
Production of objects of labour	17	15	−2

Source: as in preceding Table.

The Twelfth Plan further envisages an increase in the productivity of labour to 20-23 per cent as against 16.5 per cent in the Eleventh Plan. An important fact to be noted is that the entire increment in the national income and in the output of industry and other branches of material production is to be achieved through higher labour productivity. The growth rate of manpower resources during these years will fall and amount to only 3,200,000 persons. Apart from this, the economy will make maximum utilisation of recycled resources.

The other important feature of the Twelfth Plan would be emphasis on quality of output and work. To quote from the *Guidelines:* "The improvement of the quality of output is, in the final analysis, also a question of its quantity, of saving resources and of more fully satisfying society's needs." Giving an illustration, the *Guidelines* further state: "It is well known how acute the question of tyres is in the country... the most rational way of resolving this problem is to increase the life span of tyres. To raise this indicator by 10 per cent would be tantamount to producing six million tyres annually". Thus the emphasis in the capital goods and consumer goods sector will be on quality.

The details of the 12th Plan are given in Appendix-C.

5

THE STRATEGY FOR THE ACCELERATION OF SOCIO-ECONOMIC DEVELOPMENT

The strategy to realise the high growth rates and introduce radical changes in the management of the Soviet economy were delineated by the General Secretary of the CPSU Central Committee Mikhail Gorbachev in his *Political Report to the 27th Congress of the CPSU*. The new economic strategy as propounded in the Political Report has been described as the "strategy of accelerating the country's socio-economic development".

Acceleration, of course, means increasing the rate of economic growth but in the Political Report parlance it goes beyond simple increase in economic growth. "In substance", says the Report, "it means a new quality of growth — an all-out intensification of production on the basis of scientific and technological progress, a structural reconstruction of the economy, effective forms of management and of organising and stimulating labour."[1]

Moreover, the policy of acceleration is not confined to changes in the economic field. It will pursue an active social policy placing emphasis on social justice. It presupposes an improvement of social relations, a renovation of the forms and methods of work of political and ideological institutions, a deepening of socialist democracy, and elimination of inertness, stagnation, conservatism etc., which are holding back social progress.

While delineating his strategy of acceleration, Mikhail Gorbachev alluded to the shortfalls in economic development and to the widening gap between the targets and actual results. He particularly noted the fall in growth rates since the 1970s. To quote: "As a result, the targets for economic development set in the CPSU programme, and even the lower targets of the 9th and 10th Five Year Plans, were not attained. Neither did we manage to fully carry out the social programme charted for the period. A lag ensued in the material base of science and education, health protection, culture and everyday services."[2]

He also emphatically referred to the gap between the needs of society and the attained level of production, between the effective demand and the supply of goods. He also singled out the shortfall in the production of agricultural products and in some of the industries like engineering, coal, oil, electrical engineering, ferrous metals, chemicals and capital construction.

The watchword of this policy is that the people must, within a short time, feel the results of the common effort in solving the food problem, meeting the demand for high quality goods and services, improving the medical services, housing conditions, environment and so on.

The question now is, how this acceleration is to be achieved? As far as the industrial sector is concerned, achievement of acceleration involves taking simultaneously five measures.

First of all, acceleration involves changing the structural and investment policy. This envisages shifting the centre of attention from quantitative indices to *quality and efficiency* in all the stages of production, from building up production assets to renewing them, from expanding some material resources to making better use of them. What this essentially means is that emphasis will shift from fulfilling quantitative plans to quality. Until now, in their zest to fulfil their production quota the managers had been sacrificing quality for quantity. The end result was that in most cases the final product did not last long and had to be replaced within a relatively short time. This meant extra expenditure in the ultimate analysis. If the quality is good, the product or the piece of equipment would last longer leading to savings in raw materials and investment. Similarly, the increased demand for oil is to be met not by raising the flow of oil from wells or digging more wells, but by economising on the use of energy.

Keeping these goals in view, the Twelfth Plan has allocated more than 200 billion roubles — more than what had been allocated during the last ten years — for modernization and technical re-equipment of production.

Thus, secondly, the key to higher growth rates lies in the modernization of the machine building industry in the first instant: It is intended to introduce resource saving and labour saving technologies. The introduction of these types of machines is expected to result in savings equivalent to the labour of 12 million people, more than 100 million tons of fuel and so on. For instance, it has been calculated that the use of Don-1500 harvester combine will lead to a considerable reduction in the number of grain harvesting machines, will release about 400,000 machine operators, and will reduce grain losses by millions of tons.

Thirdly, acceleration will be achieved through large-scale introduction of computers and overall automation of important industries. The development of computer software and of management information systems has been put on an industrial footing. The Academy of Sciences of the USSR has set up an information science and computer technologies division to coordinate R&D. In most of the advanced countries industrial robots and computers are taking over risky and heavy jobs from men. This has not only increased the speed of production but has ensured even and high quality. Many of the industries in the USSR are using computers and robots but till last year, it had not become a mass movement.

According to an article published in the *Soviet Land* (No. 13, July 1986) during the Eleventh Plan period, the Soviet industry manufactured 60,000 numerically controlled machine-tools and 47,000 industrial robots. By the end of the Twelfth Plan, the production of such tools will reach 110,000 and that of robots will exceed 100,000. During the same period, the USSR will install about 200 flexible automated systems (including fully automatic shops and plants) and 3000 computer aided design systems.

However, this should not be construed to mean that every plant or factory or production process will be computerised or robotised. The philosophy behind the introduction of computers and robots has been best summed up by Professor Leonid Volchkevich, a specialist in automation; says the Professor, "Robots are costly. To be effective they must be used not where it is possible to use them, but where they cannot be dispensed with. In many cases, other types of equipment, such as rotor and rotor conveyor lines developed in the USSR, produce a better effect. At a little extra cost, they increase productivity by many times."

Soviet specialists believe that a lot depends on the way, new equipment is used. Experience shows that robots employed as single units, as an addition to existing plant, often function at a loss. It is necessary that they are integrated with manufacturing systems.

Soviet experts, working on the new systems, believe that an effective way of automating output is to set up automatic modules combining a variety of functions. One such instance is the use of robotised turning modules introduced last year in a machine tool plant in the city of Ryazan. One such module includes a numerically controlled machine-tool, a robot and a system for feeding blanks, as well as machinery accuracy control. This piece of equipment can operate in the automatic mode, unattended through all three shifts. Productivity in such a case is higher by 200-300 per cent when compared with traditional turning lathes. By 1990, 800 such automatic modules will be turned out by the plant.

The fourth important dimension of the acceleration programme is the radical modernisation of the fuel and energy complex. The programme lays emphasis on energy saving production methods, on the replacement of liquid fuel by natural gas and coal and the use of more sophisticated methods of oil refining. Similarly in the extraction industries, new techniques to be employed include open cast coal mining, use of hydromonitors in coal extraction and so on.

The fifth dimension relates to the technical re-equipment of the production infrastructure, priority being given to transport and communications. The measure involves coordinated developent of the country's integral transport system, improving the coordination of the work of all types of transport, eliminating unprofitable transport operations, reducing the time of the delivery of cargoes and ensuring their safety. As for the railways, the emphasis would be on modernising and replenishing the locomotive and carriage fleet by supplying it with more reliable and economical locomotives of the new series, electric and diesel trains, goods carriages of greater carrying capacity and tonnage and more comfortable passenger cars for surface and underground railways. During the next five years, it is planned to put .into operation 2,300 kilometres of new railway lines, build more than 4,000 kilometres of parallel lines of track, and electrify 8,000 kilometres of railways.

In the case of marine transport, the emphasis would be on improving the use of fleet and the capacities of ports and shipyards. In the air, transport acceleration strategy would be aided by the introduction of new, highly efficient long distance passenger planes and cargo planes of medium load-carrying capacity and so on. Similarly, a number of changes are envisaged for the river transport, motor transport, pipeline transport and industrial transport.

The other component of acceleration strategy is the special attention to be paid to the development of light industry and other industries that directly meet consumer demand. Advanced equipment for them will be manufactured not only by specialised industries but also by other industries. Not only the production targets are being raised but quality would also be the watchword, whether it is textiles and garments or durable consumer goods like TVs, refrigerators, washing machines, sewing machines, furniture or chemical compounds like washing powders and detergents. It also involves improvement of shopping services. It is envisaged to increase the number of self-service shops, sale by catalogue and advance orders with their delivery to the buyers' homes.

The final dimension of the acceleration programme is to orient science to serve the needs of the national economy. The idea is to make the maximum use of new technologies developed in the Soviet Union.

The Soviet Union has the largest technical manpower in the world and the Soviet scientific community has patented a number of inventions and discoveries; there are a number of organizations in the Soviet Union which encourage competition among workers in the rationalization of processes or encourage them to propose innovations which lead to increased productivity or savings on fuel or raw materials.

A number of production processes and technologies patented by the Soviet scientists are being profitably used in advanced capitalist countries. Among them, USA is an important buyer of Soviet technologies. This is evident from the table on page 76.

The data in the table pertains to the year 1976. It is however reported that since 1962, the US firms have purchased twice the number of Soviet licenses than they have sold licenses of their own to the USSR. The American buyers of Soviet licenses include Kaiser Aluminium, Texas utilities, Olin Bras, Bristol-Myers and Du Pont. A few years ago Du Pont purchased the technology for the production of antiarhythmic medicine which is being marketed worldwide.

It is further reported that in the past few years, the USSR has sold 700 licenses to nearly 50 countries which include apart from USA, Germany, France, Italy, Britain, Japan, Canada and Australia. The most sought-after technologies from the USSR are for iron and steel, non-ferrous metallurgy, engineering, chemicals, pharmaceuticals, welding, etc.

For instance, the evaporative cooling blast furnance technology developed in the USSR has made it possible to utilise waste heat leading to savings in power and water consumption. This process has been acquired by Belgium, Italy, Canada, Japan, USA and Australia. Similarly "dry quenching technique" has improved the quality of coke (coal) and saves the atmosphere from pollution. This process is being used by Nippon Steel, Nippon Kokan and Ishikawajima-Harima Heavy Industries of Japan; Italimpanti of Italy; Altos Hornos of Spain; Newten Chambers of Britain; and Thyssen Engineering of West Germany.

In spite of the fact that the Soviet Union has patented a large number of processes, not many of them have been adopted by the Soviet industry. This is attributable to overemphasis on the fulfilment of production quotas. After the production quotas had been fulfilled, the managers had no incentive left for introducing new processes. In many cases, since the introduction of new equipment and new technology involved cessation of production for some time, the managers were in no mood to stop their production line for a

Publicly known Soviet technologies being used or developed for commercial application by US companies in 1976.

Area	Technology	Company
Energy	Underground coal gasification	Texas Utility Services
Medicine		
	Surgical stapling device	US Surgical
	Pharmaceutical technology	American Home Products and Dupont
	Titanium hip prosthesis	US Surgical
Metallurgy	Tube mills to produce thin-wall tubing from hard-to-work metals such as stainless steel and titanium	Carpenter Technology and Universal Oil Products
	Cored wire manufacturing process for electric welding	Chemtron
	Magnetic impulse welding for nuclear fuel elements	Maxwell laboratories
	Electromagnetic aluminium costing technique	Reynolds and Kaiser Aluminium
	Electro-slag remelting system to produce hollow steel ingots	Cabot
	Technology for the descaling of steel	Fenn Manufacturing
	Evaporation Cooling process for blast furnace	Andco
Mining	Hydraulic mining technology	Kaiser Resources
	Magnesium extraction technology using diaphragmless electrolysers	American
	Method for leaching aluminium from ore	Southwire
	Rockbreaking machine	Joy Manufacturing
Miscellaneous	Pneumatic drifter drill (hole hog) for laying underground cables without digging open trenches	Allied Steel & Tractor
	Particle accelerator	Energy Sciences

Source: Michael Ellman, *Socialist Planning*, Cambridge, Cambridge University Press, 1979, p. 53.

brief period and thereby run the risk of non-fulfilment of production quota.

This was particularly referred to by Gorbachev in his Political Report. He provides two instances where two important inventions were set aside. In the first instance, the Soviet scientists had discovered three decades ago, a fundamentally different kind of lubricant that increased the life of machine parts subjected to friction. This discovery which would have helped save billions of roubles, has to this day, not been applied on a large-scale "because of the blinkers worn by some high ranking executives of the USSR Ministry of Petrochemical Industry and also of a number of other ministries and departments."[3]

The second instance refers to the invention of "antifriction bearing" which makes machines more reliable and failure-proof under the most rigorous operational conditions. Though this was invented ten years ago, the Ministry of Motor Vehicle Industry and Planning never took cognizance of this.

Thus it is now being emphasized that all levels of economic management must change their attitude to the introduction of new methods and technology.

The acceleration strategy indicated that there would also be certain changes in the planning approach. Instead of giving rigid production quotas and balancing the demand and supply of raw materials and intermediate goods through the material balances method, it is likely that the Twelfth Plan would make more use of economic levers. For instance, instead of the GOSPLAN or Ministry of Supplies ensuring the supplies, it is the factory which will find out the source of its supply at the prices to be determined within a certain range. The two parties would enter into contract for the supply of certain good raw material or piece of equipment to be supplied in a defined period of time. Non-fulfilment of contract may carry penalty.

Similarly, the funds for investment would not just be allocated from the central budget, but will bear some real or shadow interest to make efficient use of scarce resources. As for the consumers goods, the managers will not get output targets from above which were rigid to the extent of indicating the colour and size of a particular commodity. The managers of the consumers goods industry will now have the freedom in deciding the type of their product, its quantity, or size combination. In other words the consumers goods industry is being made more responsive to the needs of the consumer.

Tackling Food Problem

In spite of heavy investments in the agricultural sector, the Soviet Union has not yet been able to completely eliminate imports of grains. As such there is nothing wrong in the import of grain to meet the domestic deficit, but it acquires political overtones when the importer happens to be a superpower and a little at "loggerheads" with the other superpower. In 1981, the Soviet Union imported food worth more than 6 billion dollars. But in the same year, the Gulf countries also imported food worth more than 6 billion dollars. The Federal Republic of Germany is the biggest importer of agricultural products in the world. In 1978, FRG imported food and food products worth 15.6 billion dollars and exported agricultural products worth 5.6 billion dollars. Thus FRG was a net importer of agricultural products to the tune of 10 billion dollars.

However, in international relations, the political overtones in trade need to be met squarely. Therefore, the 27th Congress took up the challenge seriously. As Gorbachev noted: "Comrades, a problem we will have to solve in the shortest possible time is that of fully meeting our country's needs for food." It is envisaged to double the growth rate of farm production by the application of modern intensive technologies and by improving the socio-economic conditions in the rural side and by changing the system of management. The state and collective farms will be given autonomy to choose their action plan within the broad framework of planning.

There would still be fixed plans for the purchase of produce from the collective farms and the state farms for each year of the five year period. These plans will not be altered, but the farms will be allowed to dispose of their balance produce in any manner they think fit — they may sell it to the state or to the consumer directly or sell it through cooperative outlets.

At the same time, some of the problems afflicting the agricultural sector like low productivity, structural imbalances etc., will be tackled simultaneously. Drought in recent years has become a major problem for Soviet agriculture. As a result of this, there are marked fluctuations in agricultural production from year to year which affect the supply of foodstuffs to the population and the development of the economy as a whole. It is for this reason that great attention is now being paid to the drainage and irrigation of land in the USSR. The area under irrigation, between 1970 and 1983, increased from 11 to 19 million hectares, and that of drained land from 6 million to 14.7 million hectares.[4] Though this adds upto less than 15 per cent of all arable land, it now yields one-third of agricultural output.

In 1984, the Soviet Union adopted a long-term programme for land improvement, covering the period 1986-90 and beyond, upto the year 2000. Under this programme, large-scale measures are to be implemented to increase the effectiveness of irrigated and drained land and to accelerate the development of irrigated agriculture in the south of the European part of the country, in order to create there large zones where agricultural production can be guaranteed. It is also planned to continue the development of irrigation in the Republics of Central Asia and the Transcaucasian area and to carry out a series of land-improvement measures in other agricultural zones of the USSR.

The ultimate aim of all these measures is to increase the quantity and quality of the consumption of agricultural products. According to the Food Programme, by 1990, it is planned to increase per capita consumption as follows: meat by over 20 per cent (upto 70 kg), vegetables, melons etc, by 30 to 39 per cent (upto 126-135 kg.), fruits and berries by 74-84 per cent (upto 66-70 kg). The present level of production provides 58.4 kg. of meat, but the level of money income of the Soviet population creates a demand calculated at roughly 75 kg. This is one reason why a few economists in the USSR are advocating increase in the prices of food products. One of them is Academician Abel Aganbegian, Deputy

Academic Secretary of the Economics Department of the USSR Academy of Sciences.

Prices

Along with the changes in the systems of economic management, there is also going to be a departure from the present system of rigid prices. It should not, however, be construed that market forces will have full play in the economy *a la* western capitalist countries where all investment and production decisions are based on market prices, but prices would "become an active factor of economic and social policy." The man would still be at the centre of planning and prices would be related to his incomes. Within that framework, prices would be made more flexible. As Political Report puts it: "price levels must be linked up not only with the outlays but also with the consumer properties of the goods, their effectiveness and the degree to which products meet the needs of society and consumer demands." In this sense it is planned to use the concept of ceiling prices and contract prices on a very large scale.

As far as the Soviet consumer goods industries are concerned, the concept of ceiling prices would introduce keen competition among them. If two similar goods are priced differently, then the one selling at the lower price would be sold out soon. The factory producing goods at the higher price will have no option but to reduce its cost of production. It will also have a salutary effect on the quality of the goods. The managers of the Soviet enterprises will now be on their toes to manufacture quality goods at lower costs. The central budget will not now come to their rescue in case of unsold goods. As for the fixing of ceiling price, the ***international price*** of similar goods (of similar quality) would provide the ***reference point.***

Small-scale Sector

The Political Report, also attaches importance to the role of medium and small industries. As the Report notes: "...small and well equipped plants have their own advantages in many cases. They can be quicker and more flexible in taking into account technological innovations and changes in demand, can meet faster the demand for small batch and separate items, and can make better use of available manpower, especially in small towns." In other words though the emphasis will remain on large industrial enterprises, the medium and small enterprises would also be encouraged.

References

1. Mikhail Gorbachev, *Political Report of the CPSU Central Committee to the 27th Party Congress,* Moscow, Novosti Press Agency Publishing House, 1986, p. 29, hereinafter referred to as Political Report).
2. Political Report, p. 25.
3. Political Report, pp. 32, 33.
4. V.A. Martynov, "The problems of developing the Agro-Industrial System in the USSR," *International Social Science Journal,* Vol. XXXVII, No. 3, 1985, pp. 364.

6

CONCLUSION

The Soviet economy at the moment is poised for great changes. The 27th Congress of the Communist Party of the Soviet Union has recommended a number of changes in the economic structure of the country and in the system of economic management. If one may say so the economic changes as suggested by the 27th Congress has three 'watchwords' — **modernisation, efficiency** and **responsiveness.** The Report to the Congress emphasizes **modernisation** of all the sectors of the economy, be it industry, agriculture, transport or service. Conscious efforts are to be made to introduce new efficient technologies and processes in all the sectors of the economy.

Efficiency implies that all production should be realised at the minimum expenditure of labour, raw materials and energy.

Responsiveness implies that goods will be produced which are in demand. This is particularly important for the consumers goods sector where the industrial units had concentrated on fulfilling the plan targets at the cost of quality. The result has been the pile of unsold goods. Now the industrial units manufacturing consumer goods will not get rigid plans from above but will have the freedom to manufacture goods of the kind people demand. The success of an enterprise would now be determined not on the basis of the fulfilment of the plan but on the basis of its sales. In economic terminology, as far as the consumers goods sector is concerned, there will be a shift from the present "planners' preferences" to "consumers' preferences."

These three objectives are to be realised not only through conscious efforts but also through large-scale use of economic levers such as profits, interest rates, prices, shadow prices and so on. For instance, earlier, new investments were made through central budgetary allocations. Even now the allocations will be made through the central budget but the enterprises will now have to pay same notional rate of interest to the exchequer. In the absence of such a notional rate of interest, the managers had been exaggerating their investment needs. Again, the profit earning enterprises could make investments from their own sources without asking for budgetary allocations.

Similarly, other changes that are being envisaged relate to the introduction of 'contract system' for the supply of goods etc. Under the Material Balances system, the demand and supply were matched on paper by the GOSPLAN. In actual practice, however, there were delays in the supply of raw materials and other inputs due to a combination of internal and external factors. Now the enterprises can directly enter into contract with other enterprises for the supply of specified inputs within a stipulated time. They may introduce penalty clauses if the inputs are not made available within the specified time.

The other reform relates to the pricing structure — prices of both the capital goods and consumers goods. As far as the prices of capital goods and other industrial products are concerned, they are to be brought more in line with the international prices of similar goods; the emphasis, however, would be on manufacturing quality goods at prices lower than international prices.

Regarding the revision of the prices of consumer goods, the emphasis would be on rationalization and elimination of subsidies to the extent possible, without, however, violating the principle of social justice. One would like to quote at length the observations of Academician Abel Aganbegian on this issue:

"The price-formation system certainly needs to be improved. The direction of improvement is quite clear: prices should more closely reflect the social necessity of expenditure and more closely correspond to the effectiveness, quality and competitiveness of goods. In general, profitability of production should be determined by its benefit to society.

"Certain measures have already been taken. For example, a more effective system of price surcharges and rebates was introduced at the beginning of 1986. The prices of goods of insufficient quality and with inferior technical characteristics are now being rapidly reduced. Price reduction will continue until such goods are withdrawn from production. Contractual prices between trade and industry, for example, are being established on a much broader scale. In general, of the 24 million kinds of goods produced in this country, the prices of half a million are fixed in various centralized ways. I think it will take several years to prepare more substantial innovations in the wholesale price system.

"Economists are constantly discussing the problems in the formation of retail prices, which also need improvement. But this does not mean that any radical reforms in this sphere have been planned for the very near future.

"Proposals have been published in the press to raise the prices of bread, meat, milk and butter, whose production is subsidized by the state budget which annually allocates many thousands of millions of roubles for this purpose. From the economic point of view, this cannot be considered normal. The prices of these foods have not changed for more than 20 years.

"I personally believe that price formation demands great improvement. This could include cancelling subsidies other than those for such items as goods for children and pensioners, medicines, etc., and thus freeing funds which could be used for other social needs.

"It should be stated quite definitely, however, that if at some point such a price reform were to be carried out, in the conditions of a socialist economy such a reform would have to be combined with a compensation programme. In other words, no matter how this very complex problem is resolved, the principles of social justice will not be violated."[1]

It should, however, not be concluded, as some in the West are doing, that the Soviet Union is about to give up the planning system in favour of market economy. It may be emphasized that no free play of market forces is being envisaged; the market will not determine as to what is to be produced, where investment is to be made, who will earn how much and so on. The five year plans will be very much there, planners will indicate where the resources will go (as in the capital goods sector) but will leave the minute details to be worked out by the managers with the help of the economic levers. Social justice will continue to get the top priority.

Following chapter two, we may say that the Soviet economy is going back to the principles of planning enunciated by Lenin — principles of "democratic centralism", "directive planning", "use of economic levers", and "perspective planning".

At the moment, however, it is difficult to say what shape the economic reforms will assume, but one thing is certain that these will have a salutary effect on the Soviet economy. The next fifteen years of this decade are quite crucial for the Soviet economy.

Reference

1. Abel Aganbegian, *Make the Economy Responsive to Innovation,* Moscow, Novosti Press Agency, 1986, pp. 26-29

APPENDIX — A

THE STRATEGIC COURSE: ACCELERATION OF THE COUNTRY'S SOCIO-ECONOMIC DEVELOPMENT

Excerpts from the Political Report of the CPSU Central Committee to the 27th Congress of the Communist Party of the Soviet Union, presented by Mikhail Gorbachev

Comrades, by advancing the strategy of accelerating the country's socio-economic development at the April Plenary meeting, the Central Committee of the CPSU adopted a decision of historic significance. It won the wholehearted support of the Party, of the entire people, and is being submitted for discussion at the Congress.

What do we mean by acceleration? First of all, raising the rate of economic growth. But that is not all. In substance it means a new quality of growth: an all-out intensification of production on the basis of scientific and technological progress, a structural reconstruction of the economy, effective forms of management and of organising and stimulating labour.

The policy of acceleration is not confined to changes in the economic field. It envisages an active social policy, a consistent emphasis on the principle of socialist justice. The strategy of acceleration presupposes an improvement of social relations, a renovation of the forms and methods of work of political and ideological institutions, a deepening of socialist democracy, and resolute overcoming of inertness, stagnation and conservatism — of everything that is holding back social progress.

The main thing that will ensure us success is the living creativity of the masses, the maximum use of the tremendous potentials and advantages of the socialist system.

In short, comrades, acceleration of the country's socio-economic development is the key to all our problems: immediate and long-term, economic and social, political and ideological, domestic and foreign. That is the only way a new qualitative condition of Soviet society can and must be achieved.

A. The Results of Socio-Economic Development and the Need for Its Acceleration

Comrades, the programme tasks of the Party raised and discussed at our Congress necessitate a broad approach to the assessment of the results of the country's development. In the quarter of a century since the adoption of the third CPSU Programme, the Soviet Union has achieved impressive successes. The fixed production assets of our economy have increased seven times. Thousands of enterprises have been built, and new industries created. The national income has gone up by nearly 300 per cent, industrial production 400 per cent and agricultural production 70 per cent.

Before the war and in the early postwar years the level of the US economy appeared to us hard to attain, whereas already in the 1970s we had come substantially closer to it in terms of our scientific, technical and economic potential, and had even surpassed it in the output of certain key items.

These achievements are the result of tremendous effort by the people. They have enabled us to considerably enhance the well-being of Soviet citizens. In a quarter of a century real per capita incomes have gone up 160 per cent, and the social consumption funds more than 400 per cent. Fifty-four million flats have been built, which enabled us to improve the living conditions of the majority of families. The transition to universal secondary education has been completed. The number of people who finished higher educational establishments has increased fourfold. The successes of science, medicine, and culture are universally recognised. The panorama of achievements will not be complete if I say nothing about the deepgoing changes in social relations, the relations between nations, and the further development of democracy.

At the same time, difficulties began to build up in the economy in the 1970s, with the rates of economic growth declining visibly. As a result, the targets for economic development set in the CPSU Programme, and even the lower targets of the 9th and 10th five-year plans, were not attained. Neither did we manage to carry out fully the social programme charted for this period. A lag ensued in the material base of science and education, health protection, culture, and everyday services.

Certainly, the state of affairs was affected, among other things, by certain factors beyond our control. But they were not decisive. The main thing was that we had failed to produce a timely political assessment of the changed economic situation, that we failed to apprehend the acute and urgent need for converting the economy to intensive methods of development, and for the active use of the achievements of scientific and technological progress in the national economy. There were many appeals and a lot of talk on this core, but practically no headway was made.

By inertia, the economy continued to develop largely on an extensive basis, being oriented towards drawing additional labour and material resources into production. As a result, the rate of growth of labour productivity and certain other efficiency indicators dropped substantially. The attempts to rectify matters by undertaking new projects affected the problem of balance. The economy, despite the enormous resources at its disposal, ran into shortage of them. A gap appeared between the needs of society and the attained level of production, between the effective demand and the supply of goods.

And though efforts have been made of late, we have not succeeded in wholly remedying the situation. The output of most types of industrial and agricultural goods fell short of the targets set by the 26th Congress of the CPSU for the 11th five-year-plan period. There are serious lags in engineering, the oil and coal industries, electrical engineering, in ferrous metals and chemical industries, and in capital construction. Neither have the targets been met for the main indicators of efficiency and the improvement of the people's standard of living.

And we, comrades, must draw the most serious lessons from all this.

The *first* of them may be described as the lesson of truth. A responsible analysis of the past clears the way to the future, whereas a half-truth which shamefully evades the sharp corners holds down the elaboration of realistic policy, and impedes our advance."Our strength," Lenin said, "lies in stating the truth". That is precisely why the Central Committee deemed it essential to refer once more in the new edition of the Party Programme to the negative processes that had surfaced in the 1970s and the early 1980s. That is why, too, we speak of them at the Congress today.

The *other lesson* concerns the sense of purpose and resolve in practical actions. The switchover to an intensive development of such an enormous economy as ours is no simple matter and calls for considerable effort, time, and the loftiest sense of responsibility. But once transformations are launched, we must not confine ourselves to half-hearted measures. We must act consistently and energetically, and must not hesitate to take the boldest of steps.

And *one more lesson* — the main one, I might say. The success of any undertaking depends to a decisive degree on how actively and consciously the masses take part in it. To convince broad sections of the working people that the chosen path is correct, to interest them *morally* and materially, and to restructure the psychology of the cadres — these are the crucial conditions for the acceleration of our growth. The advance will be all the more rapid, the tighter our discipline and organisation will be, the higher the responsibility of each for his job and its results.

Today, the prime task of the Party and the entire people is to reverse resolutely the unfavourable tendencies in the development of the economy, to impart to it the due dynamism and to give scope to the initiative and creativity of the masses, to truly revolutionary change.

There is no other way. In the absence of accelerated economic growth, our social programmes will remain wishful thinking, even though, comrades, they cannot be put off. Soviet people must, within a short time feel the results of the common effort to resolve cardinally the food problem, to meet the need for high-quality goods and services, to improve the medical services, housing, the conditions of life, and environmental protection.

The acceleration of socio-economic development will enable us to contribute considerably to the consolidation of world socialism, and will raise to a higher level our cooperation with fraternal countries. It will considerably expand our capacity for economic ties with the peoples of developing countries, and with countries of the capitalist world. In other words, implementation of the policy of acceleration will have far-reaching consequences for the destiny of our Motherland.

B. Economic Policy Guidelines

Comrades, the draft Programme of the CPSU and the draft Guidelines define the main targets of our economic and social development. By the end of this century we intend to increase the national income nearly twofold while doubling the production potential and qualitatively transforming it. Labour productivity will go up by 2.3-2.5 times, energy consumption per rouble of national income will drop by 28.6 per cent and metal consumption by nearly 50 per cent. This will signify a sharp turn towards intensifying production, towards improving quality and effectiveness.

Subsequently, by intensifying these processes we intend to switch over to an economy having a higher level of organisation and effectiveness, with comprehensively developed production forces, mature socialist relations of production, and a smoothly-functioning economic mechanism. That is our strategic line.

As was emphasised at the conference in the Central Committee of the CPSU in June 1985, the main factors behind this line are scientific and technological progress and a fundamental transformation of society's productive forces. It is impossible to effect cardinal changes with the previous material and technical foundation. The way out, as we see it, lies in thorough modernisation of the national economy on the basis of the latest scientific and technological advances, breakthroughs on the leading avenues of scientific and technological progress, and restructuring of the economic mechanism and management system.

1. Modernisation of the National Economy on the Basis of Scientific and Technological Progress

The CPSU has tremendous experience in carrying out major scientific-technological and socio-economic transformations. However significant they are, the scale and complexity of the work we carried out in the past cannot be compared with what has to be done in the period ahead to modernise the national economy.

First of all, changing the structural and investment policy. The substance of the changes lies in shifting the centre of attention from quantitative indices to quality and efficiency, from intermediate results to end results, from building up production assets to renewing them, from expanding fuel and raw material resources to making better use of them, and also to speeding up the development of research-intensive industries and of the production and social infrastructures.

A big step forward is to be made in this direction in the current five-year period. It is intended to allocate upwards of 200 billion roubles of capital investments — more than during the past ten years — for modernising and technically re-equipping production. Sizeable though these amounts are, the planning and economic bodies will have to continue the search for additional resources for these purposes.

Large-scale integrated programmes in the strategic areas have been drawn up, and their implementation has begun. The industries that play the key role in scientific and technological progress, that assure a quick economic return and the solution of urgent social problems, will move ahead more dynamically. Substantial funds and material, scientific, and manpower resources are being concentrated to speed up their development.

It is clear that the effectiveness of modernisation and also the economic growth rates depend to a crucial degree on *machine-building.* This is where the fundamental scientific and technological ideas are materialised, where new implements of labour and machine systems that determine progress in the other branches of the national economy are developed. Here the foundations are laid down for a broad advance to basically new, resource-saving technologies, higher productivity of labour and better quality of ouput.

The Congress delegates know that the CPSU Central Committee and the USSR Council of Ministers recently adopted a decision on the further development of machine-building. In substance, it is a national programme for modernising this essential sector of industry. A single management body has been set up in it. The machine-building complex has been set the goal of sharply raising the technical-economic level and quality of machines, equipment and instruments already by the end of the 12th five-year plan period. The capital investments allocated for modernising this industry will be 80 per cent greater than in the previous five years.

What specifically, do we expect from the implementation of this programme? The output of machinery and equipment is to increase by more than 40 per cent, and their quality standards will be improved. The growing stream of machines of new generations will pave the way for a fundamental retooling of the national economy and a growth in its effectiveness. The resultant annual savings will amount to the labour of about 12 million people, more than 100 million tons of fuel, and many billions of roubles. Calculations show that the use of the Don-1500 harvester alone, for example, will lead to a considerable reduction in the number of grain harvesting machines, will release about 400,000 machine-operators, and will reduce grain losses by millions of tons.

Large-scale introduction of computers and comprehensive automation of production will tremendously influence the rate of technical modernisation. Concrete targets in the development and large-scale application of modern computers and expansion of the manufacture of their components have been defined. The development of computer software and of management information systems is being put on an industrial footing. The Academy of Sciences of the USSR has set up an information science and computer technologies division to coordinate research and development.

Radical modernisation of the fuel and energy complex is the keynote of the Energy Programme. The Programme puts the emphasis on energy-saving technologies, on the replacement of liquid fuel by natural gas and coal, and on more sophisticated methods of oil refining. Advanced technologies are also to be employed in the extraction industry: open-cast coal mining, the use of hydromonitors in coal extraction, the development of improved and more reliable oil extraction equipment and the universal introduction of automated systems. In the course of the current five-year period two and a half times more nuclear power plant generating capacities will be started up than in the previous five years, and outmoded units at thermal power stations will be replaced on a large scale.

A great deal will have to be done in the metal-making and chemical industries, in introducing more highly productive equipment there. The production of fundamentally new and improved structural and other advanced materials will accelerate the development of electronics, machine-building, construction, and other branches of the conomy.

The Party attaches enormous importance to technical re-equipment of the production infrastructure, in the first place, in transport and communications. Top priority will be given to the development of light industry and other industries that directly meet consumer demand. Advanced equipment for them is to be manufactured not only by specialised industries but also by other industries.

We will not be able to carry out technical modernisation unless we radically improve capital construction. This calls for raising the entire building industry complex to a new industrial and organisational level, shortening the investment cycle by a minimum of 50 per cent both in modernising enterprises and in the construction of new facilities. We cannot reconcile ourselves any longer to slow construction rates that freeze enormous sums and retard scientific and technological progress in the national economy.

All these tasks, comrades, are gigantic in scale and significance. How they are carried out will, in the final analysis, determine the fulfilment of our plans and the rates of our growth. Each sector and each enterprise must have a clear-cut programme for the continuous modernisation of production. The responsibility of the planning and economic bodies for the achievement of planned targets will increase accordingly. Party organisations should also direct their activities towards this.

It is especially important to prevent window dressing and the use of palliative instead of substantive measures. There are disquieting instances, and by no means solitary ones, of ministries and departments erecting new facilities under the guise of modernisation, of stuffing them with outdated equipment, and of drawing up costly projects that do not assure the rise of production to higher technical-economic levels.

Here is an illustration of that approach. The Bryansk Engineering Works, which puts out motors for diesel locomotives, is now in the middle of a 140 million-rouble retooling programme. What results will this modernisation of capacities yield? It turns out that the programme does not provide for the introduction of advanced technologies, the number of workers has already been increased by nearly 1,000, and the return on the assets has dropped. The worst part of it is that they intend to use the new capacities to manufacture an outdated motor, although a more efficient model has been designed and tested.

What does the stance of the executives of the Ministry of the Heavy Machine-Building Industry and of the Ministry of Railways mean? Evidently some comrades have failed to grasp the profound importance of the task confronting them. Such facts deserve stern condemnation as undermining the Party's policy of modernisation and of accelerated scientific and technological progress. Such cases should be examined with all severity.

The need for modernisation poses new tasks for *scientific research.* The CPSU will consistently pursue a policy of strengthening the material and technical base of scientific research to the maximum, of providing scientists with the conditions for fruitful work. However, our country is entitled to expect, from its scientists, discoveries and inventions that will bring about genuinely revolutionary changes in the development of machinery and production methods.

Important measures to make the work of research establishments more effective have been outlined lately. They deal with incentives for scientists and new forms of interaction between science and production. A decision was recently adopted to set up inter-sectoral research-and-technological complexes, including the large institutes that are leaders in their respective fields, among them institutes under Academies of Sciences, design organisations and pilot plants.

Steps are also being taken to intensify the work of sectoral research institutes and to increase their contribution to speeding up scientific and technological progress. However, this process is going ahead at an impermissibly slow pace. Many institutes are still an appendage of ministry staffs; not infrequently they support departmental interests and are bogged down in red tape and paper-work. The question of bringing science close to production, of including sectoral research institutes into production and research and production associations, was forcefully raised at the June conference. We must ascertain who is opposing this, what stand the ministries and their Party committees take on this issue, and how they are reacting to life's demands.

The research potential of higher educational establishments must also be used more effectively. Upwards of 35 per cent of our country's research and educational personnel, including about half of the holders of doctoral degrees, are concentrated there but they carry out no more than ten per cent of the research projects. The respective departments should draft and submit proposals for strengthening the links between university research and production. The proposals should also take into account the training of the next generation of researchers. Just as a forest cannot live on without undergrowth, a true scientist is inconceivable without students. This is a question of the future of science, and, therefore, of our country, too. Beginning with their freshman year, college and university students should be drawn into research work and into participation in applying research findings in production. This is the only way that real scientists and creatively-thinking specialists can be trained.

In sum, comrades, the orientation of science towards the needs of the national economy should be carried out more energetically. However, it is equally important to orient production towards science, to make it maximally receptive to scientific and technological advances. Regrettably, no few scientific discoveries and major inventions fail to find practical application for years, and sometimes for decades. I shall cite a few examples.

The non-wear and tear effect, which Soviet scientists discovered three decades ago, led to the development of fundamentally new lubricants that greatly increase the service life of machine parts subjected to friction and sharply reduce labour outlays. This discovery, which may yield a saving of many millions of roubles, has not yet been applied on a broad scale because of the inertness of some high-ranking executives of the USSR Ministry of Petrochemical Industry and of a number of other ministries and departments.

The Ministry of the Motor Vehicle Industry and planning bodies are to blame for the fact that for about ten years now a newly-invented anti-friction bearing, which makes machines more reliable and failure-safe under the most rigorous operating conditions, has not been applied on a large scale. The Ministry of the Machine-Tool Industry has impermissibly held up the manufacture of unique hydraulic motors enabling extensive use of hydraulic techniques in mining and elsewhere, to increase labour productivity several-fold and to improve working conditions.

Unfortunately, this list could be continued. This kind of attitude to new inventions is not infrequently based on the ambitions of some groups of scientists, on departmental hostility towards inventions made "by others", and a lack of interest on the part of production managers in introducing them. It is no secret that even the examination of invention applications is sometimes an ordeal that drags on for years.

We cannot reach our targets in accelerating scientific and technological progress unless we find levers that will guarantee priority only to those research establishments and industrial enterprises whose work collectives actively introduce whatever is new and progressive and seek ways and means of manufacturing articles of high quality and effective yield.

We have already accumulated a definite amount of experience in improving the economic mechanism in the sphere of science and its interaction with production. It must be thoroughly analysed and then applied without delay, closely linking up material incentives for research collectives and individual researchers with their actual contribution to the resolving of scientific and technological problems.

At all levels of economic management there should be a new attitude to the introduction of new methods and technology. This also refers to the State Planning Committee of the USSR, which should go over more boldly to all-inclusive planning of scientific and technological progress, as well as to the USSR State Committee for Science and Technology, which is reorganising its work too slowly. The Academy of Sciences of the USSR, ministries, and departments should pay more attention to basic research and to applying its findings in production. This is a sacred duty of every scientist, engineer, designer, and manager of an enterprise.

Our activity in the sphere of *foreign economic contacts* must be tied up more closely with the new tasks. There should be a large-scale, forward-looking approach to mutually advantageous economic relations. The member-countries of the Council for Mutual Economic Assistance have worked out a policy of this kind. It presupposes a switchover in economic relations among them from primarily trade relations to deeper specialisation and cooperation in production, above all, in machine-building, and to the establishment of joint associations and research-and-production complexes.

We have no few departments and organisations that are responsible for separate spheres of foreign economic relations but they do not always coordinate their work. In setting the aim of actively using foreign economic contacts to speed up our development we have in mind a step-by-step restructuring of foreign trade, of making our exports and imports more effective.

2. *Solving the Food Problem : A Top-Priority Task*

Comrades, a problem we will have to solve in the shortest time possible is that of fully supplying our country with food. This is the aim of the Party's present agrarian policy, formulated in the decisions taken by the CPSU Central Committee at its May 1982 Plenary Meeting and in the Food Programme of the USSR. In the period since their adoption a good deal has been done to expand the material and technical base of agriculture and of the related industries. The economy of the collective farms, state farms, inter-farm enterprises and processing plants has become stronger; the productivity of crop-farming and livestock farming has risen.

There is progress, but the lag in agriculture is being overcome slowly. A decisive turn is needed in the agrarian sector to improve the food supply noticeably already during the 12th five-year plan period. It is planned to more than double the growth rate of farm production and to ensure a substantial increase in the per capita consumption of meat, milk, vegetables, and fruit.

Can we do this? We can and we must. The Party has therefore worked out additional measures to raise the efficiency of all sectors of the agro-industrial complex. Their substance consists in changing the socio-economic situation in the rural areas, in creating the conditions for greater intensification and guaranteed farm produce. The emphasis is put on economic methods of management, broader autonomy of collective farms and state farms and their higher responsibility for the results of their work.

In carrying out this policy we will have to make more effective use of the production potential in the agro-industrial complex and concentrate efforts and resources on the most important sectors providing the highest returns. It is a question, first and foremost, of increasing soil fertility and creating the conditions for stable farming. As the experience of recent years has shown, the key to success lies in large-scale application of intensive technologies. They have a tremendous effect. Their application made it possible to obtain, last year alone, an additional 16 million tons of grain and a substantial amount of other produce.

Reducing losses of farm produce during harvesting, transportation, storage, and processing is the most immediate source of augmenting food stocks. We have no small potentialities in this respect; an increase in consumption resources could amount to as much as 20 per cent, and in the case of some products to as much as 30 per cent. Besides, eliminating the losses would cost two to three times less than supplying the same amount of produce.

The Central Committee and the Government have now defined major steps to reduce losses. Rapid expansion of agricultural machine-building will make it possible to equip the collective farms and state farms with highly productive machines capable of performing all the field jobs faster and better. We have also made additional outlays to increase the manufacture of machinery for the food industry and facilities for the processing and storage of food.

The Party and the state will persistently continue to strengthen the material and technical base of the agro-industrial complex. It is equally clear, however, that people will, as before, be the mainspring and inspiration of progress. Today, more than ever before, agriculture needs people who want to work actively, who have a high level of professional skill and a feeling for the new. Constant attention to the working and living conditions of the people in rural areas is the best guarantee of all our successes. All our plans are geared to this, and it is important that they should be carried out unswervingly.

All these are urgent measures, but the programme of action is not confined to them. The switchover of the agrarian sector to new methods of administration and management has to be completed. The establishment, in the centre and in the localities, of unified management bodies of the agro-industrial complex, called upon to carry out genuine and effective integration of agriculture and of the related industries, is undoubtedly a step of fundamental significance.

The establishment of this organisational framework is backed up by an effective economic mechanism. Proposals on this score have already been drafted. The main idea is to give broad scope to economic methods of management, to substantially broaden the autonomy of collective farms and state farms, to increase their interest in and responsibility for the end results. In substance, it is a question of creatively applying, in the conditions of today, Lenin's idea of the food tax.

It is intended to establish fixed plans for the purchase of produce from the collective farms and state farms for each year of the five-year period; these plans will not be altered. Simultaneously, the farms will be given the opportunity to use all the produce harvested over and above the plan, and in the case of fruit and potatoes and other vegetables a considerable part of the planned produce, as they see fit. The farms can sell it, additionally, to the state, can sell it, either fresh or processed, on the collective-farm market or through cooperative trade outlets, or use it for other needs, including the needs of personal subsidiary holdings. Additional allocations of material resources for which there is a heightened demand, and also other incentives, will encourage farms to sell grain to the state over and above the plan.

In future, the republics, territories, and regions will be given fixed quotas for the delivery of produce to centralised stocks; everything produced over and above that will be kept for the local supply system.

There is to be a transition to improved planning methods based on advanced standards. The role of cost accounting will be substantially increased. Past experience shows that neglect of the principles of self-support, material interest and responsibility for performance led to a deterioration of the financial and economic position of collective farms and state farms and also to their considerable indebtedness. Genuine cost accounting, with the incomes of enterprises depending upon the end results, should become the rule for all links of the agro-industrial complex and, first and foremost, the collective farms and state farms. The contract and job-by-job systems of payment at the levels of teams, groups, and families to whom the means of production, including land, will be assigned for a period specified by contract, will become widespread.

There will be big opportunities for displaying initiative and resourcefulness. This also presupposes, however, a higher sense of responsibility for meeting the targets of the Food Programme, for the results of the financial and economic activity of collective farms, state farms, inter-farm enterprises and organisations. A reliable barrier must be erected in the way of mismanagement and parasitism, and an end must be put to excuses such as "objective circumstances", which some collective farms and state farms have been using to cover up their ineptitude and sometimes a lack of desire to work better. The farms will have to use chiefly their own funds to develop production, increase profits and incomes and provide incentives. The practice of providing bank loans will have to be substantially altered to stimulate a higher level of activity of collective farms and state farms.

As you see, comrades, conditions for rural economic management are undergoing a cardinal change. This calls for major changes in the style and methods of guidance of the agro-industrial complex. An end must be put to incompetent interference in production activity in rural areas. We expect the State Agro-Industrial Committee of the USSR and its local bodies to do everything so that our country receives weighty returns from the measures that are being taken.

3. Economic Management Must Measure Up to the New Demands

Comrades, the new economic tasks cannot be solved without an in-depth readjustment of the economic mechanism, without creating an integral, effective and flexible system of management that will make it possible to take fuller advantage of the possibilities of socialism.

It is obvious that economic management requires constant improvement. However, the situation today is such that we cannot limit ourselves to partial improvements. A radical reform is needed. Its meaning consists in truly subordinating the whole of our production to the requirements of society, to the satisfaction of people's needs, in orienting management towards raising efficiency and quality, accelerating scientific and technological progress, promoting a greater interest of people in the results of their work, initiative and socialist enterprise in every link of the national economy, and, above all, in the work collectives.

The Central Committee of the CPSU and its Political Bureau have defined guideliens for reorganising the economic mechanism. We set ourselves the aims of:

— heightening the efficiency of centralised guidance of the economy, strengthening the role of the centre in implementing the main goals of the Party's economic strategy and in determining the rates and proportions of national economic growth, its balanced development. Simultaneously, the practice of interference by the centre in the daily activities of the lower economic links must be overcome;

— resolutely enlarging the framework of the autonomy of associations and enterprises, increasing their responsibility for attaining the highest ultimate results. Towards this end, to transfer them to genuine cost accounting, self-support and self-financing., and to make the income level of collectives directly dependent on the efficiency of their work;

— going over to economic methods of guidance at all levels of the national economy, for which purpose to reorganise the system of material and technical supply, improve the system of price formation, financing and crediting, and work out effective incentives to eliminate overexpenditure;

— introducing modern organisational management structures, taking into account the trends towards concentration, specialisation and cooperation of production. This is a question of setting up complexes of interconnected industries, research and technological inter-sectoral centres, various forms of economic associations and territorial-production associations;

— ensuring the best possible combination of sectoral and territorial economic management, integrated economic and social development of republics and regions, and the organisation of rational inter-sectoral contacts;

— carrying out all-round democratisation of management, heightening the part played in it by work collectives, strengthening control from below, and ensuring accountability and publicity in the work of economic bodies.

Comrades, we now unquestionably stand before the most thorough reorganisation of the socialist economic mechanism. The reorganisation has begun. The direction along which work is going ahead in the agro-industrial complex has been already spoken about. Management of the machine-building complex is being upgraded. Industrial enterprises are being transferred, in the main, to a two-level system of management. Beginning with the current year, new economic management methods which have gone through experimental testing have been introduced in enterprises and associations that turn out half of the total industrial output. Their introduction in the service sphere, in construction and in transport has begun. Collective forms of organising work and providing incentives, and economic contract systems are being applied on an ever wider scale.

We are only at the beginning of the road, however. Time and energetic efforts are needed to reorganise the economic mechanism in our country with its vast and complex economy. Difficulties may arise, and we are not guaranteed against miscalculations either, but still the main thing now is to move ahead purposefully, step by step, along the direction we have chosen, supplementing and perfecting the economic mechanism on the basis of the accumulated experience and eliminating everything that has outlived itself or has failed to justify itself.

Success will depend largely on the *reorganisation of the work of the central economic bodies, first and foremost, the State Planning Committee of the USSR*. It must indeed become our country's genuine scientific and economic headquarters, freed from current economic matters. We have begun this work. New management bodies of the intersectoral complexes are being set up, and the major part of the day-to-day management functions is being delegated directly to the enterprises and associations. The State Planning Committee and other economic agencies must concentrate their efforts on long-term planning, on ensuring proportional and balanced economic development, on carrying out the structural policy, and on creating the economic conditions and incentives for attaining the best end results in each unit of the national economy. Considerable improvements are needed in the sphere of statistics.

Lately there has been a weakening of the *financial-credit influence on the economy*. The financial system does not sufficiently stimulate higher economic efficiency. The defective practice of income redistribution, with the losses of lagging enterprises, ministries and regions covered at the expense of those that operate profitably, has reached a large scale. This undermines cost accounting, promotes parasitism and prompts endless demands for assistance from the centre. Crediting no longer serves its purpose.

"Any redical reforms", said Lenin, "will be doomed to failure unless our financial policy is successful". Accordingly, we must radically change the substance, organisation and methods of the work of the financial and credit bodies. Their chief aim is not to exercise petty control over the work of enterprises but to provide economic incentives and to consolidate money circulation and cost accounting, which is the best possible controller. Everything must be made dependent on the end result. The question of improving collection of the turnover tax, deductions from the profit and other budget revenues has obviously come on the agenda. Their size and the procedure for their payment should more effectively help reduce losses in production, raise quality of output and promote its sale.

Prices must become an active factor of economic and social policy. We shall have to carry out a planned readjustment of the price system as an integral whole in the interests of organising effective cost accounting and in conformity with the aims of increasing the real incomes of the population. Prices must be made more flexible; price levels must be linked up not only with the outlays but also with the consumer properties of the goods, their effectiveness and the degree to which products meet the needs of society and consumer demand. Ceiling prices and contract prices are to be employed more widely.

The system of *material and technical supply* also needs thorough improvement. It must be turned into a flexible economic mechanism which helps the national economy to function rhythmically and steadily. It is the direct duty of the State Committee for Material and Technical Supply to contribute actively to the establishment of direct long-term relations between producers and consumers on a contractual basis, and to improve the observance of the terms of delivery. Wholesale trade in the means of production should be developed.

In the final analysis, everything we are doing to improve management and planning and to readjust organisational structures is aimed at creating conditions for the *effective functioning of the basic link of the economic system : the association or enterprise.*

As shown by analysis, the results of the experiments that have been carried out could have been much better, if, on the one hand, there had been a corresponding reorganisation of the work of industrial ministries and central economic agencies, which continue their attempts to restrict the powers of enterprises, and, on the other hand, if the incentives for higher efficiency had been brought home to every section, work team and workplace. Special attention should be paid to this.

It is high time to put an end to the practice of ministries and departments exercising petty tutelage over enterprises. Ministries should concentrate their attention on technical policy, on intra-sectoral proportions, and on meeting the requirements of the national economy in high-quality products put out by their respective industries. Enterprises and organisations should be given the right independently to sell to one another what they produce over and above the plan, as well as raw and other materials, equipment, etc., which they do not use. They should also be given the legal right to make such sales to the population. What sense is there in destroying or dumping onto waste heaps articles that could come in useful in the household, in building homes, garages or cottages on garden and vegetable plots?

It would be difficult to overestimate the role of economic *standards*. When the work collectives of enterprises know, ahead of time, specifics of the planned period — delivery targets, prices, deductions from profits to the budget, standards for forming wage funds and cost-accounting incentives funds — they can draw up creatively plans which provide for higher production growth rates and much higher efficiency without being afraid to reveal their as yet untapped potentialities. Moreover, enterprises should be given the possibility — following the example of the Volga Auto Works and the Sumy Engineering Works — themselves to earn the funds needed to expand and retool production.

It is especially important to give enterprises and organisations greater autonomy in the sphere of consumer goods manufacture and services. Their task is to react quickly to consumer demand. It is along these lines that we are reshaping the economic mechanism of light industry. The range of targets approved from above is being sharply limited for enterprises in this sphere; their plans will be drawn up, chiefly on the basis of contracts with trade organisations, which, in turn, must see to it that their orders conform to the actual consumer demand. In other words, the quantity, range,and quality of goods, that is, just what people need, will be the main thing, and not gross output. Besides, it is planned to establish inter-sectoral production and industrial-commercial associations for the manufacture and sale of light industry goods and to open more retail outlets operated by them.

The time has also come to solve another problem. An enterprise's wage fund should be directly tied in with the returns from the sale of its products. This will help to exclude the manufacture and supply of low-grade goods for which there is no demand, or, as they say, production for the warehouse. Incidentally, that approach should be applied not only in light industry. We can no longer reconcile ourselves to a situation in which the personnel of enterprises producing worthless goods lead an untroubled life, drawing their full pay and receiving bonuses and other benefits. Indeed, why should we pay for work which produces goods nobody wants to buy. One way or another all this goes against us, comrades ! We must not forget about this.

A well-thought-out approach must also be taken to the question of a rational combination of *large, medium and small enterprises*. As experience shows, small, well-equipped plants have their own advantages in many cases. They can be quicker and more flexible in taking into account technological innovations and changes in demand, can faster meet the demand for small-batch and separate items, and can make better use of available manpower, especially in small towns.

Another substantial aspect of readjustment is consolidation of the territorial approach to planning and management. This is especially important for our vast and multinational country with its diverse features. The actions of ministries and departments that neglect the conditions in and the requirements of regions, with resulting economic imbalances, were rightly criticised at Party conferences and at congresses of the communist parties of constituent republics.

Some suggestions are also being received on this score. It is evidently worthwhile giving thought to enlarging the powers of republican and local bodies — following the example of the agro-industrial complex — in the management of construction, inter-sectoral production units, the social and production infrastructures, and many consumer goods factories. The work of the State Planning Committee of the USSR and of the ministries should get broader territorial orientation. The question of national-economic management on the basis of large economic areas deserves study.

Our short and long-term plans are linked, to a considerable degree, with the tapping of the natural wealth of Siberia and the Soviet Far East. This is a very important matter that requires a statesmanlike approach ensuring integrated regional development. Special attention should be paid to providing people there with the conditions for fruitful work and a full-blooded life. That is the main question today, and fulfilment of the set targets depends on how it is solved.

Attention should be drawn at our Congress to the problems involved in the further socio-economic development of the Non-Black-Earth Zone of the Russian Federation. I will stress two points. The Central Committee of the CPSU and the Soviet Government have adopted special decisions for an upswing in the agriculture of the Non-Black-Earth Zone, and they must be carried out unswervingly and fully. That is in the first place. And in the second place, the local Party, government and economic bodies and work collectives must pay much more attention to making effective use of the potential accumulated there and of the allocated resources.

Consolidation of the territorial principle of management calls for a higher level of economic guidance in each republic, region, city, and district. Proposals that come from the localities are at times not thought out thoroughly, not dictated by the interests of the national economy but rather by a dependant's mentality and sometimes even by self-seeking interests, which draw the economy into capital-intensive and low-productive projects. Due attention is not paid everywhere to raising the efficiency of production. In Kazakhstan, for example, the share of national income per unit of fixed production assets is a third less than the average for the Soviet economy. In Turkmenia, the productivity of social labour has not grown at all in 15 years. Thought should be given as to how to tie in the resources allocated for social needs more closely with the efficiency of the regional economy.

Comrades, every readjustment of the economic mechanism begins, as you know, with a readjustment of thinking, with a rejection of old stereotypes of thought and actions, with a clear understanding of the new task. This refers primarily to the activity of our economic personnel, to the functionaries of the central links of administration. Most of them have a clear idea of the Party's initiatives, actively support them, boldly tackle complicated assignments, and seek and find the best ways of carrying them out. This attitude deserves utmost support. It is hard, however, to understand those who adopt a wait-and-see policy or who, like the Gogol character that thought up all kinds of fanciful ideas, do not actually do anything or change anything. There will be no reconciliation with the stand taken by functionaries of that kind. We will simply have to part ways with them. All the more so do we have to part ways with those who hope that everything will settle down and return to the old lines. That will not happen, comrades!

In our work on restructuring the economy and the economic mechanism it is more important than ever to rely on science. Life prompts us to take a new look at some theoretical ideas and concepts. This applies to such major problems as the interaction of the productive forces and the production relations, socialist ownership and its economic forms, commodity-money relations, the coordination of centralism with the autonomy of economic organisations, and so on.

Practice has revealed the insolvency of the ideas that under the conditions of socialism *the conformity of production relations to the nature of the productive forces* is ensured automatically, as it were. In real life, everything is more complicated. Indeed, the socialist production relations open up broad vistas for development of the productive forces. However, they must be constantly improved. And that means outdated economic management methods must be noticed in good time and replaced by new ones.

The forms of production relations and the economic management and guidance system now in operation took shape, basically, in the conditions of extensive economic development. These gradually grew out of date, began to lose their stimulating effect and in some respects became a brake. We are now striving to change the thrust of the economic mechanism, to overcome its costliness and to orient it towards a higher level of quality and efficiency, acceleration of scientific and technological progress and enhancement of the human factor. This is the main thing that will, in practice, signify further improvement of the socialist production relations and will provide new scope for the growth of the productive forces.

In this work we must not be stopped by long-established ideas, let alone by prejudices. If, for example, it is necessary and justifiable to apply economic standards instead of targets that are sent down as directives, this does not mean a retreat from the principles of planned guidance but only a change in its methods. The same can be applied to the need to broaden the autonomy, initiative and responsibility of associations and enterprises, and to enhance their role as socialist commodity producers.

Unfortunately, there is a widespread view when any change in the economic mechanism is regarded as practically being a retreat from the principles of socialism. In this connection I should like to emphasise the following: socio-economic acceleration and the consolidation of socialism in practice should be the supreme criterion in the improvement of management and of the entire system of the socialist production relations.

The *aspects of socialist property* as the foundation of our social system acquire great relevance. Socialist property has a rich content; it includes a multi-faceted system of relations among people, collectives, industries and regions of the country in the use of the means of production and its results, and a whole range of economic interests. This complex of relations requires a definite combination and constant regulation, especially since it is in motion. Unless we gain a deep understanding of these changes in theoretical terms we cannot arrive at correct practical decisions and consequently take prompt steps to mould a genuine sense of responsibility to socialist property.

We must provide the working people with greater incentives for putting the national riches to the best possible use and multiplying them. How can this be done? It would be naive to imagine that the feeling of ownership can be inculcated by words. A person's attitude towards property is shaped, first and foremost, by the actual conditions in which he has been put, by his possibilities of influencing the organisation of production, and the distribution and use of the results of work. The problem is thus one of further intensifying socialist self-government in the economic sphere.

The role of work collectives in the use of social property must be raised decisively. It is important to carry out unswervingly the principle according to which enterprises and associations are wholly responsible for operating without losses, while the state does not bear any responsibility for their obligations. This is where the substance of cost accounting lies. You cannot be a master of your country if you are not a real master in your factory or collective farm, in your shop or livestock farm. It is the duty of the work collective to answer for everything, to multiply the social wealth. Multiplication of the social wealth, as well as losses, should affect the income level of every member of the collective.

And, of course, a reliable barrier is needed against all attempts to extract unearned income from the social property. There are still "snatchers", persons who do not consider it a crime to steal from their plant everything that comes their way, and there are also sundry bribe-takers and grabbers who do not stop at using their position for selfish purposes. The full force of the law and of public condemnation should be applied to all of them.

Attention should also be paid to such a topical problem of regulating socialist property relations as ensuring unquestionable priority of the interest of the whole people over the interests of industries and regions. Ministries, departments and territorial bodies are not the owners of means of production but merely institutions of state administration responsible to society for efficient use of the people's wealth. We cannot allow departmental and parochial interests to hinder realisation of the advantages of socialist property.

We also stand for full clarity on the question of cooperative property. It has far from exhausted its possibilities in socialist production, in providing better satisfaction of people's needs. Many collective farms and other cooperative organisations are managed effectively. And wherever the need exists, utmost support should be given to the establishment and growth of cooperative enterprises and organisations. They should become widespread in the manufacture and processing of products, in housing construction and in construction on garden and vegetable allotments, and in the sphere of services and trade.

It is also time to overcome prejudices regarding *commodity-money relations* and underestimation of these relations in planned economic guidance. Refusal to recognise the importance of their active influence on people's interest in working better and on production efficiency leads to a weakening of the cost-accounting system and to other undesirable consequences. Conversely, sound commodity-money relations on a socialist basis can create a situation and economic conditions under which the results depend entirely on the standards of the work done by the collective and on the ability and initiative of the managers.

Thus, comrades, we are obliged to assess the situation again and again and to resolutely reorganise everything that has become out of date, that has outlived itself. A profound understanding of this task by Party activists and by all personnel, as well as its comprehension by the broad masses are indispensable for success, are the point of departure in the exceptionally important work of building up a new economic mechanism and management system.

4. Putting Reserves of Economic Growth into Action

Comrades, the Party has worked out a strategy of deep-going transformations in the national economy and has begun to effect them. They will undoubtedly enable us to speed up economic growth. As was noted, however, this will require a good deal of time, but we must increase the growth rates at once, today. The specific feature of the 12th five-year plan period consists in retooling the national economy on a new scientific and technological basis while simultaneously stepping up the rates of our advance.

Hence the need to utilise all of our reserves to the maximum. It is more sensible to start with those that do not require big outlays but yield quick and tangible returns. This is a matter of economic-organisational and socio-psychological factors, of making better use of the production capabilities that have been built up, of making the incentives more effective, of improving the level of organisation and tightening discipline, and of eliminating mismanagement. Our reserves are at hand, and with a dedicated approach plus good management they promise high returns.

Just look at the capacities in operation. The value of our country's fixed production assets exceeds 1.5 trillion roubles, but they are not all being used properly. This applies to a number of industries — to machine-building, heavy industry, the power industry and agriculture. What is especially alarming is the fact that the most active assets — machinery, equipment, and machine-tools — often stand idle or else are operated at half capacity. In the engineering industry, for example, metal-cutting machine-tools are in use only slightly more than one shift a day. On the whole, our country annually loses billions of roubles worth of industrial output because capacities are underloaded. Planning and economic bodies and work collectives at enterprises must do everything possible to ensure the operation of existing capacities at the designed level. In heavy industry alone, this would nearly double the output growth rates.

Failure to meet component delivery obligations is another hindrance. A violation of this kind in one place has a ripple effect throughout the national economy and lowers its efficiency. Jerky production also does tangible damage. It is no secret that at the beginning of the month many plants stand idle longer than they function. But at the end of the month they begin a headlong rush, as a result of which output quality is low. This chronic disease must be eradicated. Strict observance of component delivery obligation is the duty of work collectives and also of management at all levels. We will not be able to achieve our aims unless we bring order into planning and supply, create the necessary stocks, and impose higher financial liability at all levels for failure to meet obligations and for spoilage.

There are also great reserves in the use of manpower. Some economic managers complain of a manpower shortage. I think the complaints are groundless in most cases. If you look into the matter more closely you will see that there is no shortage of labour. But there is a low level of labour productivity, inadequate work organisation and ineffective incentive schemes. Add to this the creation of superfluous jobs by planning and economic bodies. It is a well-known fact that some of our enterprises, design offices and research institutes have considerably larger staffs than their counterparts abroad with the same work load.

Once people at enterprises get down in earnest to improving work organisation and incentives, to tightening discipline and setting higher demands, reserves that had never been thought to exist previously are brought to light. Application of the Shchokino method and the certification of work places convincingly confirm this. When Byelorussian railwaymen went over to new pay system, with one person doing two or more different jobs, about 12,000 workers were soon freed for jobs in other sectors.

Of course, more attention must also be paid to production mechanisation and automation. In tackling this problem one does not have to wait for machines and devices to be designed and made somewhere else. A great deal can be accomplished by using one's own capabilities. For instance, efforts in this direction in Zaporozhye Region led, in three years, to a nine per cent reduction in the number of workers employed in manual jobs in industry and a fifteen per cent reduction in the number of those in similar jobs in the building trades. I think that other regions, territories, and republics have no fewer possibilities. The important thing is to put persistent and dedicated effort into this, showing consideration for the people who have to perform manual operations, and striving to reduce production outlays.

Generally speaking, comrades, there are enormous economic reserves. We have not yet really begun to use many of them. The mentality of a substantial section of the managerial personnel at various levels took shape against the background of an abundance of resources. Many were spoiled by these riches, and that led to wastefulness. However, the situation changed long ago. The former influx of manpower has dwindled, and we have begun to pay a heavy price for every ton of oil, ore, and coal we extract and deliver. We cannot close our eyes to these facts; we must reckon with them. We must economise everywhere and always: on the job and at home. We must not ignore mismanagement and wastefulness. Nearly the whole of this year's growth in the national income is to come from raising labour productivity and lowering materials and energy consumption.

That is not simple but wholly feasible. All the more so since our country has accumulated experience in making thrifty use of resources; but it is not being spread fast enough. Party, YCL, and trade union organisations should constantly promote thrift and encourage those who make economical and rational use of raw materials, electrical energy, and fuel. We must make it a firm rule that overexpenditure of resources is disadvantageous and savings are tangibly rewarded.

I would like to put special emphasis on the problem of *output quality standards.* This is more than our immediate and major reserve. Accelerated scientific and technological progress is impossible today without high quality standards. We are sustaining great material and moral losses because of flaws in design, deviations from technology, the use of low-grade materials and poor finishing. This affects the precision and reliability of machines and instruments and hinders satisfaction of consumer demand for goods and services. Last year millions of metres of fabrics, millions of pairs of leather footwear and many other consumer items were returned to factories or marked down as inferior-grade goods. The losses are significant: wasted raw materials and wasted labour of hundreds of thousands of workers. Radical measures must be taken to rule out the manufacture of defective or low-grade goods. The full force of pecuniary and administrative influence and legislation must be applied for this purpose. There is also evidently a need to adopt a special law on the quality of output.

Recently the Central Committee of the CPSU called upon

Party committees, government and economic bodies, trade union and YCL organisations and all working people to make maximum efforts to radically improve the quality of goods. This must be a matter of concern for every Communist, for every Soviet citizen, for all who respect their own work, for all who cherish the honour of their enterprise, their industry, and the honour of our country.

A great deal of important and intensive work lies ahead of us. The first year of the five-year plan period is a year of persistent work, a year of tests for every manager and work collective. We must pass this test, draw all the reserves of the economy into production, and consolidate the foundation for further transformations.

The industry and talent of Soviet citizens are the key to attaining the goal that has been set. It is now up to efficient organisation and precise direction of this great force. The part to be played by socialist emulation in this effort cannot be overestimated. It should be spearheaded at raising the standards of work, economising and thriftiness, and reaching the targets set before each collective and at each workplace. Enthusiasm and the growing skills have been and, we are confident, will continue to be our reliable support.

C. The Basic Guidelines of Social Policy

Comrades, questions of social policy, concern for man's welfare, have always stood at the centre of our Party's attention.

The social sphere encompasses the interests of classes and social groups, nations and nationalities, the relationship between society and individual, the conditions of work and life, health and leisure. *It is the sphere in which the results of economic activity affecting the vital interests of the working people are realised, and the loftiest aims of socialism are carried into effect. It is the sphere in which the humanism of the socialist system, its qualitative difference from capitalism, is seen most distinctly and graphically.*

Socialism has eliminated the main source of social injustice — the exploitation of man by man, and inequality in relation to the means of production. Social justice reigns in all areas of socialist social relations. It is embodied in the real power of the people and the equality of all citizens before the law, the actual equality of nations, respect for the individual, and conditions for the all-round development of the personality. It is also embodied in broad social guarantees — employment, access to education, culture, medical care and housing, concern for people in old age, and mother and child welfare. Strict observance in life of the principle of social justice is an important condition for the unity of the people, society's political stability, and dynamic development.

But life, as they say, does not stand still. So we must look at the further development of the social sphere with new eyes, and appreciate the full measure of its increasing significance. We are obliged to do so in keeping with the general course worked out by the Party for the acceleration of socio-economic development, and with the programme aim of our Party, that of achieving the complete well-being and a free all-round development of all members of society.

Lessons of the past, too, require that we pay greater attention to social issues. The Party's Central Committee holds that central and local bodies had underestimated relevant problems concerning the material base of the country's social and cultural sphere. As a result, a residual principle had actually taken shape governing allocation of resources for its development. There was a certain overemphasis on technocratic approaches, blunting attention to the social aspect of production, to everyday life and leisure; this could not but reduce the interest of the working people in the results of their work, slacken discipline and lead to other negative developments.

We are not at all indifferent to what ways and means are used to improve the material and spiritual aspects of life and what social consequences this entails. If private-owner, parasitic sentiments, and levelling tendencies begin to surface, this means that something is wrong about the choice of ways and means in our work, and has got to be rectified. During the discussion of the pre-Congress documents, Party members and non-members spoke with concern of the slackening of control over the measure of labour and consumption, of infringements of socialist justice, and of the need for stepping up the fight against unearned incomes. The gravity and importance of these questions is more than obvious.

In short, the attained level of development and the magnitude of the new tasks call for a long-term, deeply considered, integral, and strong social policy that would extend to all aspects of the life of society. It is essential for the planning and management bodies, for central and local economic organisations to deal resolutely with the needs of the social sphere.

The objectives of social policy are thoroughly characterised in the drafts of the Party programme and the Guidelines. Allow me to dwell on some issues related to its implementation.

1. Steady Improvement of the People's Standard of Living, Consistent Application of Social Justice

The long-term plans for the country's social and economic development envisage *raising the people's well-being to a qualitatively new level.* In the coming fifteen years, the volume of resources allocated for the improvement of the conditions of life is to be doubled. Real per capita incomes are to go up 60 to 80 per cent. The rise in incomes in the 12th five-year period is to cover millions of people. Huge funds are being earmarked for increasing the construction of homes and social and cultural facilites. Those are the plans. But we must mention the main thing : these plans will become reality only if every Soviet person works hard and efficiently. This applies to every person wherever he may work and whatever post he may occupy. What we accomplish is what we are going to have, and how we are going to live.

Socialist transformations have radically changed both the purpose of work and the attitude to work of the mass of workers and peasants. This is vividly reflected in the massive growth of socialist emulation. Relying on its wealth of experience, the Party intends to continue promoting these traditions, and to cultivate a conscious and creative attitude to work as the prime duty to society.

At election meetings and conferences, Communists have rightly raised the question of not only improving the forms of moral incentives, but also of greatly increasing material incentives and establishing due order in this important matter. It was rightly pointed out that the so-called "figure juggling", payment of unearned money and unmerited bonuses, and setting "guaranteed" pay rates unrelated to the worker's contributed work, are impermissible. It should be said quite emphatically on this score that when equal payments are fixed for the work of a good employee and that of a negligent one this is a gross violation of our principles. And first of all it is an intolerable distortion of socialism's basic principle: "From each according to his ability, to each according to his work", which expresses the substance of the social justice of the new social system.

It is essential that the government's wage policy should ensure that incomes strictly correspond to the quantity and quality of work done. Proceeding from this, the increase of wage rates and basic salaries of factory and office workers in productive fields envisaged in the 12th five-year period will be enacted for the first time essentially at the expense and within the limits of the sums earned by the enterprises themselves. This procedure will make a more active impact on the acceleration of technical progress and on heightening the efficiency of production.

Rates and salaries in the non-productive sphere will go up, drawing on centralised sources. A phased increase of the salaries of doctors and other medical workers was started last year. The increase of the rates and salaries of those employed in public education is to be completed in 1987, and a start is to be made that year in raising the salaries of cultural workers. Measures are being taken to extend the wage and salary advantages of factory and office workers in cerain regions of Eastern Siberia and the Soviet Far East.

Many proposals made by working people refer to the role of social consumption funds in enforcing the principle of justice. These funds already account for nearly one-third of the consumed material goods and services. We hold that they are in no way charity. They play an important role in providing equal access for members of society to education and culture, equalising conditions for the raising of children, and easing the life of those who may, for one reason or another, need a grant or continuous assistance. At the same time, it is a means of encouraging and stimulating qualified, conscientious work. The Party intends to continue promoting the further growth and more effective use of these social funds. In the 12th five-year period they are to go up by 20 to 23 per cent.

Combatting unearned incomes is an important function of the socialist state. We must admit today that owing to a slackening of control and for a number of other reasons groups of people have appeared with a distinct proprietary mentality and a scornful attitude to the interests of society.

Working people have legitimately raised the question of rooting out such things. The Central Committee agrees completely with these demands. It is considered necessary, already in the immediate future, to carry out additional measures against parasites, plunderers of socialist property, bribe-takers, and all those who embarked on a path alien to the work-oriented nature of our system. We should also give thought to proposals about perfecting our tax policy, including the introduction of a progressive inheritance tax.

But while combatting unearned incomes, we must not permit any shadow to fall on those who do honest work to earn a supplementary income. What is more, the state will promote various forms of satisfying popular demand and providing services. We must attentively examine proposals for regulating individual labour. It stands to reason that such labour must be in full conformity with socialist economic principles, and rest on either cooperative principles or on contracts with socialist enterprises. Society, the population only stand to gain from this.

All the efforts to perfect the distributive relations will have little effect and the objective of enhancing the people's well-being will not be attained if we fail to *saturate the market with diverse goods and services*. That, indeed, is the purpose of the Comprehensive Programme for the Development of the Production of Consumer Goods and the Services.

In the current five years it is planned to secure higher growth rates for output of consumer goods and retail trade, and to considerably improve the organisation of trade and public catering. Heavy industry has been instructed to involve all enterprises in the production of manufactured goods and to ensure output of high-quality materials and equipment for light industry and the food industry.

We must build up an up-to-date services industry as quickly as possible. That is the job of central organisations, but also — no less,and perhaps even more — of the Councils of Ministers of Union Republics, and all bodies of local government. Resolute measures must be taken to eliminate the glaring disproportions between the supply and demand of services. This applies first of all to services that lighten domestic work and those connected with the improvement and renovation of flats, with tourism, and the servicing of cars the demand for which is increasing at an especially swift rate. Responding to the proposals of the working people, we are promoting broad expansion of collective gardening and vegetable growing. This has got off the ground. But the work must be continued, and all artificial obstacles must be removed.

The social importance and acuteness of the *housing problem* have predetermined our serious attitude to it. To provide every family with a separate flat or house by the year 2000 is, in itself, a tremendous but feasible undertaking. In the current five years, and especially in the five-year periods to follow, the scale of house-building and of modernising available housing will increase. The building of cooperative and individual housing should be encouraged in every way. There are great reserves here for expanding the building of homes. Those who are backing the construction of youth complexes are doing the right thing. The motivation and energy of young people can do a lot in this respect.

Much is being said about the need for seriously improving the practice of distributing housing. These questions must be settled on a broad democratic basis and put under continuous public control. Proposals for fair changes in the system of house rents by gearing them to the size and quality of all the occupied living space merit attention. There have been many complaints about the low quality of house-building. It is essential to work out measures that would stimulate a substantial improvement of quality, and also an improvement of the layout, the amenities, and architecture of our towns and villages.

Comrades, the qualitative changes in the social sphere are

impossible without *deep-going changes in the content of labour*. The main role here is to be played by the technical reconstruction of the economy: mechanisation, automation, computerisation and robotisation which, as I want to stress specially, must have an explicitly clear social orientation. Already in the current five years it is planned to sharply reduce the share of manual labour, and by the year 2000 to bring it down in the productive sphere to 15-20 per cent, relieving millions of people of manual operations. The further change of labour in the context of the scientific and technological revolution sets high demands on education and the professional training of people. In substance, the task of *establishing a single system of continuous education* is now on the agenda.

In recent years, the Central Committee has taken important steps in that direction. A reform has been launched of the *general and vocational school*. It should be said that the rate and extent of the measures taken under the reform are not satisfactory as yet. A more profound approach is required to the study of the scientific basis of contemporary production and of the leading trends of its intensification. And what is especially urgent is that all pupils should learn the use of computers. In sum, it is essential that the Leninist principle of combining education with productive labour should be implemented more fully, that the effectiveness of education should be considerably raised, and that radical improvements should be carried out in the training of young people for independent life and labour and in bringing up politically conscious builders of the new society.

The Party is setting the task of *restructuring higher and specialised secondary education*. In recent years, the growing output of specialists was not accompanied by the requisite improvement in the quality of their training. The material base of the higher school is lagging behind gravely. The use of engineers and technicians must be considerably improved.

At present, proposals have been drawn up to alter the prevailing situation. It is in the interests of society to raise the prestige of the work of engineers. The structure of higher and specialised secondary education is to be revised, so that the training of specialists will be abreast of the times and they acquire substantial theoretical knowledge and practical skills. The relationship of higher educational institutions and specialised secondary schools with various branches of the economy should evidently follow new lines, and their mutual interest in raising the level of training and retraining of cadres, in cardinally improving their use in production, should be enhanced.

Nothing is more valuable to every person and, for that matter, to society than health, *The protection and improvement of the health of people* is a matter of cardinal importance. We must consider the problems of health from broad social positions. Health depends above all on the conditions of work and life, and on the standard of living. It stands to reason, of course, that the public health service is also of tremendous importance. We must meet the needs of the population in high-quality medical treatment, health protection and pharmaceuticals as quickly as possible, and, moreover, everywhere. All this puts the question of the material and technical base of the health service in a new way, calling for the solution of many urgent scientific, organisational, and personnel problems, Considerable funds will be needed, of course, and we must see to it that they are made available.

It has long since been noted, and most aptly, that health cannot be bought in a pharmacy. The main thing is a person's way of life and, among other things, how sensibly and wholesomely a person uses his or her spare time. The opportunities for this are at hand, but the organisational side of the matter is very poorly run. Much depends on the initiative of the public, on people's avocational activity. But in towns and villages, and within work collectives, they often wait for instructions and count on assistance from above. Why do we make poor use of what is already at our disposal — of palaces, clubs, stadiums, parks, and many other facilities? Why don't the Soviets, the trade unions, and the Komsomol tackle these questions properly? Why not start a movement for more active building of simple playgrounds and gymnasiums on the residential principle? And finally, why not organise sports, tourist and other clubs on a cooperative basis?

A fight has been mounted across the country against hard

drinking and alcoholism. In the name of the health of society and of the individual we have taken resolute measures and started a battle against traditions that were shaped and cultivated over the centuries. While we should have no illusions about what has been accomplished, we can safely say that incidents of drunkenness on the job and in public places have become fewer. The situation within families is improving, the number of industrial injuries has gone down, and discipline has been tightened. But extensive, persevering and varied efforts are still needed to secure a final break with prevailing habits. There must be no indulgence here!

We face the acute task of ensuring the *protection of nature and rational use of its resources*. Socialism, with its plan-governed organisation of production and humane world outlook, is quite capable of creating a harmonious balance between society and nature. A system of measures to that effect has already been implemented in our country, and quite considerable funds are beng allocated for this purpose. There are also practical results.

Still, in a number of regions the state of the environment is alarming. And the public, notably our writers, are quite right in calling for a more careful treatment of land and its riches, of lakes, rivers, and the plant and animal world.

Scientific and technical achievements are being introduced much too slowly in nature protection. The projects of new and the reconstruction of operating enterprises are still being based on outdated notions, with wasteless and low-waste production techniques being introduced on too small a scale. During the processing of minerals, most of the extracted mass goes to waste, polluting the environment. More resolute economic, legal and educational measures are required here. All of us living today are accountable to our descendants and to history for the environment.

APPENDIX — B

MAJOR OVERHAUL A MUST — IT CONCERNS EACH AND EVERYONE

Following is the full text of the speech delivered by Mikhail Gorbachev, General Secretary of the CPSU Central Committee, at a meeting of the Khabarovsk Territory Party activists on July 31, 1986.

Dear Comrades,

I'd like to extend to you, the activists of the Khabarovsk Territory Party Organisation, heartfelt greetings on behalf of the Party Central Committee.

Our today's meeting completes my tour of the Far East. It was short; seven days are by no means enough for a tour of such a vast region, even for two territories. And yet it was useful and meaningful with its numerous meetings, conversations, and opinions exchanged. From this angle I can say that I'm satisfied with my visit to the Far East. I spent these days here with much interest, and, I believe, with much benefit for the cause. I had many meetings and conversations in Vladivostok, Nakhodka, Komsomolsk-on-Amur, and Khabarovsk. New ideas and opinions are being expressed on the way our plans are going both in the country as a whole, and in its specific regions.

First of all I'd like to say that everything which we have seen and heard these days confirms once again that the Soviet people have met the party-advanced measures with profound satisfaction, taking them close to heart, and have enthusiastically responded to the decisions adopted. I haven't heard a single negative opinion on what the Party did since the April Plenum of its Central Committee or on what it has been doing since its 27th Congress. This is, Comrades, the main political conclusion which I make on the results of my stay in the Far East.

Our people link their hopes and plans with the decisions of the 27th Congress, with the policy which the Party formulated at it. They hope that the work for the course elaborated by the Party Congress will exert a tremendous influence on the destiny of the country, and, hence, on our entire society, on work collectives, on each family and each person. This means that we managed to set forth, on the basis of a thorough, serious, and responsible scientific analysis of the realities of our society, a policy which the people have perceived as their own. This is, Comrades, a big deal, a major earnest of success in our further efforts to ensure higher activity of all public forces, of the entire political and intellectual potential of our society.

Neither the working class, nor the peasants, nor technical or creative intelligentsia want to live in the old way, to accept what is out of date, what impedes our advance and casts gloom on our reality, our life, our socialist system. We won't be able to live in the old way any longer. This is self-evident, and in this sense we can say that a certain step in acceleration has been made.

However, there is a risk that this first step may be interpreted as success, as evidence of our control of the entire situation. I said this in Vladivostok, and I'd like to say it again in Khabarovsk. Such a conclusion would be a big mistake, a delusion. We cannot be satisfied in any way with what has been achieved. In general, we should not allow our heads to be turned by success. We should know this well. This is a lesson of the past, at least of the last two decades. And now intoxication with success is especially dangerous.

Profound changes in quality, which would have consolidated the trend towards accelerated growth, have not taken place so far. Generally speaking, Comrades, we have a big and intensified work lying ahead. Let's be frank about it — the most important is yet to be done. This is something that the Party activists of our country, all Party members should understand well. I think the activists of the Khabarovsk Territory Party Organisation do understand this well.

The growth of the economic potential should be

necessarily accompanied by a large-scale improvement of planning, administration, and the style of management, by a search for new ways and methods of developing production. Neither anyone in Khabarovsk, nor in Moscow, the ministries, the State Planning Committee, the Government or Politbureau, has any ready-made recipes for achieving acceleration.

We should learn on the move tackling new tasks. And we should not be afraid of a bold advance, of risk and responsibility. We should overhaul everything on the go, so to speak, actively aiming at economic and social targets.

In recent times I have often had occasion to speak about remodelling. I touched on it almost in every conversation here, in Vladivostok and Komsomolsk-on-Amur. Some people may ask: aren't we becoming tiresome on that score?

The answer is a resolute "no", Comrades. We are doing this with good reason, Such an approach is prompted by the very logic of our development, by the vital need. After all, we are talking of exceptionally serious and important processes for our country. Too much depends on success in the remodelling to allow our attention to it to slacken even by one iota.

Let's recall what energy and zeal our Party displyed when carrying out transformation at the crucial stages of our socialist history. How many speeches and articles Vladimir Lenin wrote to explain to the people the new approaches to the building of socialism, the new economic policy when the need to introduce it was put on the agenda, the restructuring of government work at a new stage. The same applies to the Party's approach to decision-making in the First Five-Year Plans, and in the post-war years of economic recovery and development.

The scale of transformation which we are planning today is no smaller. The current restructuring covers not only the economy, but all aspects of public life — social relations, the political system, the cultural and ideological sphere, the style and methods of Party work, and all our cadres. Overhaul is a very meaningful word. I'd put an equation mark between the words overhaul and revolution. Our transformation, and the reforms mapped out in the decisions of the April Plenum of the Party Central Committee and its 27th Congress are a real revolution in the entire system of societal relations, in the minds and hearts of people, in the psychology and interpretation of the modern period, and, above all, the tasks engendered by rapid scientific and technical progress.

The CPSU, and the nation as a whole, unanimously believe that the answers to the questions set by life should be sought not outside socialism, but within the framework of our system by revealing the potential of the planned economy, socialist democracy, culture and the human factor, by relying on the initiative of the masses.

Some people in the West do not like that. They keep waiting for something which would mean a departure from socialism. They want us to go and pay our respects to capitalism, to borrow its methods. We receive a good deal of "advice" from abroad on how we should move and where. Different provocatory broadcasts are being made and articles published to cast aspersions on the ongoing changes in our country, to set the nation and the leaders of the Party at loggerheads. Such unseemly attempts are doomed to failure. The interests of the Party and the people are inseparable; our choice and political course are firm and unshakeable. The people and Party are unanimous on that main point.

But we should not allow the old dogmas to blind us, to prevent us from moving forward, creatively developing and acting on theory at this specific stage in the history of our society. We cannot allow that to happen, either.

I speak about this also because there are, of course, people in this country for whom the word overhaul is difficult to understand, and even to pronounce at times. They often fail to see what this process of renovation is all about, and perceive it as all but a shake-up of the foundations, a disavowal of our principles. Our political line is aimed at fully revealing the potentialities and advantages of the socialist system, at removing all the obstacles to our onward movement at giving full play to the factors of social progress.

And here's one more point I'd like to make. The more we advance on the road of restructuring, the more its complexity becomes obvious, and the fuller the tremendous scale of the work lying ahead is revealed. We are coming to see more and more clearly the extent to which many views of the economy, management, and social issues, statehood and democracy, education and moral standards are lagging behind the requirements and tasks of our development today, not to mention tomorrow's.

We shall have to overcome, step by step, the problems that have built up in every area of public life, to get rid of whatever has outlived itself, boldly adopting creative solutions.

The Central Committee understands that this will take a great effort and quite a long time to do. But there can be no execuse for being too slow, let alone inactive in this situation. That is why we are coming back over and over again to the need for an allround readjustment, and we will go on doing that until we assure a breakthrough, above all, in the thinking of our executive personnel, in the thinking and in the mentality of all working people of the community as a whole.

By the way, and I've seen this here, on Far Eastern soil once more, our Soviet people are for the readjustment heart and soul. What preoccupies them most, as I've seen from the letters I've been getting and from my contact with people right now, is that we should not ease off all of a sudden somewhere. That is what worries them. That means, working people are for the readjustment. Well, that is the best possible situation for the Party and for our personnel, Comrades.

The experience already at hand — I've seen it here again, — shows that the process of readjustment must go on both from above and from the grass roots. It is expected to embrace every echelon of management, every department of political and government leadership, and dock with the readjustment in production groups.

Some have been asking from time to time what's that readjustment about, how should we understand it and "what kind of dish is it"? Well, we are all "for it", but we do not know what we must do. That is exactly what many are saying.

We, in the Central Committee and in the Politbureau, think that everyone must set about the readjustment and do the whole work of readjustment by readjusting himself, first and foremost, by making clear where he stands as a citizen, by stepping up his political activity and efficiency in his area of employment, developing a greater sense of responsibility for the job he is entrusted to do and for overall performance. That must be perfectly clear, I think. Plain common sense indicates that we must not start looking around, up or down, or sideways. We must, first of all, commit ourselves to doing everything honestly, with a great sense of responsibility to ourselves and to the people. Once that is all done, the readjustment will succeed. No one can and no one must stay out of the process of acceleration of the social and economic development of our society.

But the readjustment means more than that. It implies creating such an atmosphere in society as would induce people to overcome the inertia and indifference that have built up and to get rid, in their work and in their lives, of everything that does not square with the principles of socialism, with our world outlook and our way of life. Frankly speaking, there is something here to work on. But in this case, too, everyone must first look at his own self, Comrades, whether in the Politbureau or in the primary Party organisations, everyone must do something concrete to set his house in order. We have got used to certain things in the years gone by, due to insufficient criticism, too little public information and a lack of responsibility, to things that do not respond to the principles of socialism at all. I mean both rank-and-file workers and officials. Both of them have to shake off the "cockleshells", clean themselves, as it were. And the Party Committees must do all they can to help this process.

We are carrying through this readjustment in an involved and strained international situation. Imperialism keeps on escalating the arms race, so we must build up our defence, and that requires a good deal of resources and efforts. So from this point of view, acceleration is vital.

From every point of view there is one answer: we must carry on with this readjustment persistently. That is why, above all, Comrades, there had to be the June Plenary Meeting of the Central Committee which enabled us to move on to an important stage of post-Congress work, and made it more dynamic, more aggressive, more business — like and more down-to-earth.

In this country, with its planned economy and a particular system of economic management, a land where the Communist Party is the ruling party, much, and, indeed, in decisive measure, depends on how this Party acts, how its forces, and above all the hard core work. They, our forces, and our hard core must keep everything within their field of vision and generate new ideas and devise new modes of approach, they have to be at the head of the nation-wide effort to implement the decisions of the Party Congress. I would use a good word from the history of our Party, applying it to the present situation, to the place and role of our forces and of the hard core. Today, they are the commissars of the present stage in the advancement of socialism.

Everyone must work harder. I emphasise, everyone, Comrades: those engaged in production and those engaged in science, administration, organisational and political work. We must look and see now, in relation to every sector and every enterprise, what must be done in plain terms to promote the progress of high technology, to ensure the qualitative aspect of acceleration, for, after all, it is advancing the economy that is the key task. Switching it over to a new track, to that of acceleration, with qualitatively new modes of approach, will have tremendous political, social and other consequences.

The Party has done quite a few good things over the years. We have to take that into account. But, Comrades, the present time and priorities are quite different. There will be no advance if we seek the answers to new questions in economy and technology by looking back on the experience of the '30s, '40s, '50s and even '60s and '70s. The times are different now, and so are the demands, the requirements, and also the opportunities. We must all grasp that well.

I am drawing your attention today to the progress of high technology, the application of up-to-date processes, and the new machinery of economic management. They yield the best economic effect compared with other activities. The investment in process modernisation takes, as a rule, between a year and eighteen months to pay off. But a simple expansion of production with the technical facilities unchanged and with technology of the same standard, takes between five and seven years to pay off. That is why there is so much struggle on the technology front all over the world. Technology is effectively speeding up the pace of advance of any society, enhancing the productivity of labour and yielding a quick and immense return.

We, Comrades, (I spoke about it at the June Plenary Meeting and I hope you remember it) made a serious mistake when the guidepost we went by in many areas of our science and technology policy was an average technical standard and repetition of the same solutions, and so we based our new industrial projects on the old types of machinery. Now, that machinery, while the projects were still in our long-lasting process of construction, was morally falling out of date altogether. That is to say we were building up a backward tendency. That was a serious mistake. We must radically correct it now. I have said it already openly and straightforwardly in front of the Party and the people, and I do not want to repeat myself.

Ministries, departments and enterprises are putting the finishing touches to their modernisation scheme under the 12th Five-Year Plan. We have had all the ministries reconsider all their technical projects — both for new enterprises and those to be modernised, in particular, and to stop actual implementation of whatever falls short of the present standards. For it we were now to carry through the projects with inferiority planned in advance, and go on building them as we did, you may well imagine what that would mean: we would condemn ourselves to lagging behind for 15-20-25 years. There will be no breakthrough. We have to bide our time for a year or two, complete the major engineering projects, that is those we have set out towards with emphasis on new types of machinery and new technology, before launching the new ones. But the work of the ministries on top must be backed up with that of our staff and Party organisations at local level. Some are counting on partial solutions, proceeding from their own particular problems and from their own particular view of their respective enterprises. We must put an end to that delusion, Comrades.

If, for example, in the light industry, we install the machinery we are turning out today (not all of it, of course, is bad, but much of it is), garment production and other sectors of the light industry will be putting up their productivity and quality by 3, 4, 5 and up to 10 per cent. But if we change over to new types of machinery, to be produced by the capacities we are now creating at our factories, the same enterprises, without any extension and with the same workforce, we can achieve a rise of at least 30-40-50 per cent. That is what choosing the right track in technical policy means. Please note that. We must be bold enough to undertake fundamental modernisation and to see which projects are outdated, have to be revised or halted altogether.

We have told our ministers: you have to get down to the full-scale intensification of production. We must effectively correct those who stick to old technology and old methods, and if it doesn't work, if anybody proves to be so stubborn and die-hard that you just can't budge him from his moorings and pull him out of that trench of bygone concepts, we have to part company and let him stay back while the nation will be moving ahead.

Let me say frankly that our opinion, the opinion of the Politbureau, is this: those who are prone to sponging and complaining all the time that they have too little of this and too little of that, that they want this, that and the other thing, and that it is the builders and everybody else who are to blame, and there are some causes beyond their control that prevent them from working better must give way to new forces who understand the call of the times and are ready to shoulder the tremendous responsibility.

In the next five years we will make dramatic headway in machine-building. The results, however, will be felt in some cases in two to three and in others in even three to four years. We can't make it overnight, so to speak. We must improve our production performance on the basis of thoroughly thought-out organisational and technical decisions and the use of near-lying reserves and opportunities. I have visited your enterprises here, and like in the industry of other parts of the country, one can clearly see vast idle opportunities. I have come to see clearly that you have quite a lot of difficulties, too. So you need help.

The government and the State Planning Committee are

drafting a resolution now on measures to ensure comprehensive development of the productive forces of the Far Eastern economic region.

There are provisions for fuller and more comprehensive use of the raw-material base in non-ferrous metallurgy, the timber and fishing industries of the Far East by developing complementary processing facilities. Measures are planned to strengthen the heat- and power-supply industries and to develop the transportation system, including railways and highways, ports, inland water and air transport. There are also plans to enhance the production potential of construction organisations. I would say that this will to a large extent decide the pace of general changes in the Far East.

The draft resolution pays primary attention to the social sphere. It provides for higher rates and a broader scope in the construction of housing, child-care centres, hospitals, out-patient clinics, polyclinics and schools. Large funds are being allocated to these measures.

It must be noted right here, however, that without proper organisational work for the resolution, it will have the same fate as the previous ones which, incidentally, were adopted at your requests. The unsatisfactory situation in many areas is associated precisely with poor implementation of the projected measures and unsatisfactory use of the available reserves and opportunities. You must attend more closely to economic problems and analyse all developments and facts in depth and in line with modern requirements.

Your territory is a very important industrial region of the Far East and has a considerable material and technical potential. You have a high standard of personnel training, with nearly 40 per cent of the people engaged in your economy having a higher or specialised secondary education. More than 50 per cent of your certified specialists have engineering and technical training. The territory is rich in natural resoruces. So, much more annoying is the fact that a large share of these benefits do not duly serve economic and social progress.

Your territory is packed with enterprises representing various branches of machine-building. Development is particularly fast in such priority directions as machine-tool engineering, the electrotechnical industry and heavy electrical engineering. The country receives from you high-productive automatic turret lathes, technological equipment for foundry shops, diesel engines and generator and various cranes which are all in great demand. The power transformers and various cable products manufactured in your territory practically fully meet the demand of all regions of the Far East for such products.

However, the attainment of the high projected targets and the course on intensification call for more and, specifically, for acceleration. And this means that there can be no complacency in the face of shortcomings.

It is abnormal that the greater part of new transfer lines and machine-tools are used to stock up new plants and production facilities and less to replace operational stock. At the end of the previous Five-Year Plan the rate of equipment replacement decreased, while the rate of old equipment withdrawal has dropped from 3.7 to 3.5.

All this could not but affect the five-year results. Production growth is behind the rates of growth in the fixed production assets. With the 40 per cent growth of fixed assets in the 11th Five-Year Plan, the capital productivity has decreased by 14 per cent. Now, count the effect for the nation of such use of the great potential which is at the disposal of the workers in the Khabarovsk Territory.

There has also been a decline in the share of top-quality products in the general industrial output of the territory in the 11th Five-Year Plan. The economic executives have grown used to a situation where consumers accept everything for lack of something better. But what about conscience in this case and the country's need for more cost-effective, reliable and higher-quality products? There are many enterprises which have been putting out the same products manufactured by the same old methods for 10 or even 15 years, and not really caring. I will put it straight for you: the managers in this case should not be paid anything, since everything is done by the workers. After all, the primary responsibility of the director and of the whole managerial staff to the country is to satisfy the demand for ever new economical and reliable products meeting the highest requirements. That's where their responsibility lies.

There are unpardonable delays in introducing new production facilities and the utilisation rate is often too low. This refers to 70 per cent of the industrial works commissioned or modernised over the past ten years. This means that all the new assets, and here I provisionally refer to the assets which have been in service for up to 10 years, are used just badly, while the old assets do not secure the desired efficiency and, consequently, quality for the simple reason that they are worn out, and involve repeated repairs, manpower and cost overruns and downtime. Are these the approaches on which to make progress and to secure acceleration?

For example, yesterday we visited an exhibition and I asked about the rate of utilisation of transfer lines. It proved to be 50 per cent. Transfer lines, or the things which boost labour productivity, are used to only half capacity! So where is the Party attention and control supposed to prick awake the conscience of some of our executive workers?

In 1975, or more than ten years ago, the Bikinskaya knitwear factory was put into operation. However, even ten years later it is running at only 40 per cent of its capacity. This means that our money there lies idle. With the design personnel number of 1,240, the factory employs only 520 workers or only 40 per cent of the required work force. The principal explanation for the factory's poor performance is the shortage of manpower and specialists. But has this transpired only now? This must have been known all along. This means that the initial design should have provided both for the construction of production facilities and for the establishment of an adequate social groundwork. What kind of a saving policy is this? It is the reverse of a saving policy and an insult to that notion. They have made the project cheaper by cutting off all the expenses on the development of non-productive spheres. But without this non-productive sphere the productive sphere is dead. So this means killing the whole thing. Were the local authorities and the Ministry of Textile Industry of the Russian Federation not aware of this situation from the very beginning?

In the Khabarovsk clothes association "Vostok", the rate of equipment utilisation is just above 50 per cent. This is all very wrong, Comrades. At this time and with such poignant tasks facing us such misuse of the available potential is inadmissible! Why, it needs only to be put into operation and it will secure the desired acceleration.

There are many unresolved problems in capital construction, too. In the 11th Five-Year Plan the lag from the plan in terms of introduciton of fixed assets added up to nearly one and a half billion roubles or 21 per cent. All the yearly plans for utilisation of capital investments into construction and assembly work failed. Or take the frittering away of funds and resources. At the moment there are thousands of unfinished construction projects in the territory. As a result, the volume of unfinished construction exceeds 1,100 million roubles. The construction agencies of the territory are working with a remarkable lack of rhythm. Many projects are commissioned in the second half of the year. By the results for the first six months of 1986, for example, only 16 per cent of the new fixed assets planned for the year have been commissioned. This decidedly wrong practice has long been condemned. The economic and social consequences of this kind of "management" are known only too well. This is perfectly clear to all of you.

Take the problems of development of agriculture. The Central Committee is worried that you are increasing the load on state resources with every passing year. You place demands on the centre and others, but you do not fulfil your plans and state orders although these orders are ensured by big investments and material-technical means received by the Khabarovsk Territory. Over the past five years state subsidies have increased.

Yesterday we visited the Krasnorechensky State Farm. This farm makes a good showing — it has ensured high productivity, harvests and profits. But the heads of nearby state farms were present there, and the picture at their farms is quite different — great losses, low yields of milk and poor harvests. If at all state farms milk yields were the same as at the Krasnorechensky State Farm, there would be twice as much milk produced in the Khabarovsk Territory.

Why cannot such a powerful and vast industry and economy of your territory help small-scale farming which possesses just 275,000 hectares of ploughland? The whole farm output is consumed within the Khabarovsk Territory. What hinders your progress? Parasitic attitudes, a belief that everything you need will be given and sent to you. But if all argue and act in this vein, we shall not achieve success. Of course, you will not be fully self-sufficient, but it is impermissible to justify mismanagement in the agrarian sector which is directly linked with satisfaction of the needs of the working people.

You, Comrades, should more vigorously restructure the management of enterprises and the guidance of Party organisations in the agro-industrial complex. At present good conditions have been created for developing that complex. These conditions are perhaps the most favourable as compared with other branches of the economy.

I would like to specially touch on the service sector and the output of consumer goods. This is directly linked with the Party's social policy and with invigorating the human factor, that is, with what the Party Congress has regarded as being of paramount importance. As you know, of late serious measures have been taken for stimulating the output of consumer goods not just at specialised enterprises but practically at all factories, including defence works. But the situation remains tense. Serious efforts are needed to dispel the tension and ensure a normal commodity-money turnover.

Frankly speaking, what we have heard in Komsomolsk-on-Amur is distressing or even arouses indignation. Many problems can be solved through the forces of the territory or even the city. These questions, Comrades, are of no minor importance. The living conditions of the working class tell on the productivity of labour and public sentiments. Incidentally, the people of the city themselves are offering their services. They are ready to participate if the city's authorities start ennobling the city and the recreation zone and solving other questions. They are also ready to take part in housing construction.

Today a certain investment volume has been earmarked for each region and republic. At the June Plenary Meeting we have said: ensure the fulfilment of the Five-Year-Plan with lower investment and use the funds thus released for developing the social sphere, housing stock, etc. The people of Chelyabinsk have considered the task. It has turned out that about 10 per cent of investment can be channelled from industrial construction to housing and construcion of childcare centres. Now they are solving these problems. This is one approach.

However, in Komsomolsk-on-Amur we have seen a different approach. Powerful ministries, numerous work collectives, a high concentration of the working class, but one has to wait for a flat for ten to fifteen years. Perhaps the managers of that city are present here. I feel that in general they are good and competent people. But when I think of their attitude to social problems my respect for them is diminishing. If economic executives and managers neglect the social sphere, leave it to the end, I can state point-blank that our plans will be doomed, the up-to-date production facilities — flexible and robotised production, numerically controlled machining centres, etc. — will be dead. Proper conclusions must be drawn from this, and the situation must be immediately put right.

Yesterday we saw at your exhibition how the territory will develop under the 12th Five-Year Plan. It has turned out that under the 11th Five-Year Plan your housing construction was at the level of the 10th Five-Year Plan. There was no increment. It is strange that everything was growing while the rates of housing construction remained at the same level. Childcare centres and medical establishments were built even in lower volumes. Such a policy, Comrades, cannot be tolerated.

On the whole, the social sphere must occupy a worthy place in the work of the territorial Party organisation, of all economic executives and managers. We will not be able to assure further development of the Far East without this. What is available today is not used to the full. There is no use setting up new capacities if the development of the social infrastructure of the region lags behind. We shall give some assistance to Komsomolsk-on-Amur. It is necessary to reconsider some questions, to support the city. But the main thing, Comrades, is in your hands.

I would like also to speak about the service sphere.

It is improper, Comrades, that the people of the Khabarovsk Territory receive half or a third of the services in repair and construction of dwellings, repair of footwear, manufacture of furniture, etc., that is the average for the Russian Federation as a whole. The Soviets of People's Deputies and economic managers should regard these issues as a vital task of theirs. Many managers act quite rightly when they develop the service sphere at their enterprises. This ends labour turnover, workers are optimistic and dedicated. One does not have to be a great politician to understand this.

There is much room for displaying initiative in making household chores easier, in developing tourism, in establishing a basis for sport, recreation and in promoting the cultural sphere. The Maritime and Khabarovsk Territories have unique vast opportunities for this. You, Comrades, should give proper attention to these matters. The attitude to the service sphere as to something of secondary importance must be resolutely done away with. The 27th Congress of the CPSU urged a strong social policy. Through such a policy we must invigorate the human factor and put into action the enormous potential possessed by our country, by our society. This will enable us to go ahead, to achieve acceleration. Such is the demand of the Party Congress. Such is the condition for restructuring the economy, and all of life. This is the prime and sacred task for Party, municipal and economic leaders of all ranks.

And one more point. You have not drawn the attention of a large number of industrial enterprises to the production of consumer goods. Those who avoid production of such goods must radically change their attitudes. How are you thinking, Comrades, of satisfying the market? Earnings in Komsomolsk-on-Amur are high. But the reasonable requirements of the people cannot be satisfied because there is not enough to spend the money on. One does not need to be a great expert on political economy to see and understand the situation. However, I feel I have to remind you of this.

Initiative, persistence and a search for new forms of helping the population in individual working activity are required in tackling the problems to eliminate the scarcity of goods and services. Specifically, in their letters to central bodies, many working people call for wide development of different cooperative associations and producers' cooperatives which seem to have been prematurely eliminated in the '50s and '60s.

More and more people stand for the use of auxiliary branches at enterprises of the state and cooperative sectors for providing the population with services and consumer goods. It is rightly pointed out that these branches can involve such types of raw materials and labour resources in economic turnover which today simply cannot be tapped by large enterprises. Enterprises themselves must help people. Providing workers with services by enterprises themselves must be encouraged in every way. Managers who are engaged in this deserve most vigorous support.

Let us be blunt, Comrades. The old tradition of demanding plan output persists: get on with building and producing growth. And how working people are living is a secondary consideration for some economic executives. This must be condemned proceeding from the demands of the Congress. Social problems are particularly topical here in the Far East where economic development faces a shortage of personnel. This shortage of personnel takes place because large-scale migration of the population is going on due to the absence of a real developed social sphere. Generally speaking, Comrades, we must solve these problems not after the development of production but along with the development of production. Now that production capacities have been deployed to a considerable extent, priority should be given to social problems. There can be no other way out. We must act the way Vladimir Ilyich Lenin taught us: less high-sounding phrases, twaddle, conceit, and empty theoretisation and more day-to-day concern for real deeds and meeting people's needs and requirements.

We want to step up the human factor, switching over to new forms of economic management. The Congress declared for a radical reform in management. On the instruction of the Central Committee and the government, leading scientists and experts with the participation of practical workers are drawing up an integrated concept for perfecting the system of management. Integration of leadership in branches and sub-branches will go on. Economic sub-units and management bodies oriented to the final product needed by society will be set up. The functions and status of central economic agencies will shortly be specified. I mean the State Planning Committee, the State Committee for Material and Technical Supply, the State Committee for Science and Technology, and others.

Our country and its economy are vast. Our people live and work in variegated conditions. Here in the Far East, one perhaps not only perfectly understands but just feels that it is simply impossible to manage all this vast economy only from the centre and that much of the responsibility for the solution of numerous problems has to be shifted onto local bodies. This means they should be provided with appropriate rights.

One week ago the CPSU Central Committee, the Presidium of the USSR Supreme Soviet, and the USSR Council of Ministers adopted a resolution on measures to continue raising the role and responsibility of the Soviets. You have, probably, familiarised yourselves with the summary of the resolution. If you carefully study it, you will see that the Soviets are provided with many rights. We will continue following this path. The Soviets should display their potential. But I would single out two points in this connection. Formerly we also took good decisions though they were, maybe, a little weak and less specific. But those resolutions did not always work. Why?

The thing is that local Party bodies took excessive care of the Soviets and assumed the solution of many problems for which the Soviets must be responsible. This is in the first place. Furthermore, economic executives did not have due respect for the Soviets. They did not care if a Soviet demanded developing municipal transport, extending purification installations, providing amenities for the city, building houses and community facilities, etc. Many simply turned their back on the persistent and righteous demands of the Soviets. We must get rid of this. In their activities the Soviets carry into life the very social policy which enables the people to judge about our policy in general, about its aims and priorities, and about how it serves man's needs. It is vital,

Comrades, to back this resolution and enable the Soviets to launch their work and be exacting to them.

As for the operation of enterprises under the new conditions, we are now developing a new economic mechanism, switching over on a large scale to the principles of cost accounting, self-funding, and team contract and thus adapting our enterprises to actually new conditions of work. The operating resolution on the socialist enterprise (association) has become obsolete to a considerable degree. Elaboration is nearing completion of a new law on the socialist enterprise (association). It is called upon to juridically record the line towards restructuring management methods and shielding work collectives from unnecessary tutelage and sheer administration.

Prerequisites will thus be created for effective operation of the main economic link on the basis of full cost accounting, self-funding, and socialist self-government, including the establishment of enterprise councils in the same way as team councils are set up.

I would like to know your opinion. Should the draft of this law be promulgated? (Voices: Yes, right, it would be fine).

I will report on your opinion to the Politbureau. I think we should take such a step. It is very important.

One more point, Comrades. The development of people's creative activity, raising of responsibility for the job entrusted to one, and the strengthening of discipline and order in the country are closely linked with two such serious things as the development of democracy in the country and continued implementation of the principles of social justice. The people have responded to the Party's calls and are joining in the real process not only in work collectives but within the framework of the social process in general. This should be welcomed.

I say frankly. Our Party, government, and economic personnel must learn to work under the conditions of extending democracy, stepping up the human factor, and developing people's initiative. To tell the truth, some of our personnel have resented people's over-sensitive reaction to the processes taking place in society. Some of the unquiet but interested people believing in our system and ideology and worrying about the success of the cause have often been labelled as demagogoes. Various mechanisms were invented to get rid of such people but in such a way as to get around accusations that criticism had been suppressed.

It is now vital to ensure everywhere people's real participation in running production affairs and solving the problems facing the cities, regions, territories, and society in general. Of course, demagogues may avail themselves of the democratisation. But there are very few of them. Most people want a healthy social atmosphere. They want the leaders to be closer to the working people, to ask their advice, to report back to them and to tell them what is happening. They want the leaders to strive to make all things clear and to enable each citizen to say what he feels deep down.

Lenin used to say that an illiterate person stands outside politics. Now we have made our country the most literate in the world. People's desire to participate in the management of public and state affairs is natural. Everybody must realise this and rebuild his thinking and approaches. The methods in work of the leaders of Party bodies must be such as to rely on these people's activeness, political as well as labour. There may be useful proposals. There may be proposals to act on which the conditions are not ripe; then stand up and say that.

Generally, Comrades, the style of work has to be changed. It must be imbued with respect for the people, their opinion and with a real, not sham, closeness to them. Actually reaching out listening to, meeting with and informing citizens — is what we need. And the harder the job in hand, the more often we must meet with them, be with them when a task is being solved. Our citizens are responsive; they're a remarkable people, without any parallel anywhere. The greatest staying power marks them, and they show the biggest political activeness. And it is now on the rise. This must be welcomed and encouraged in every way. Let us hold that we have agreed about this in the Khabarovsk Party branch.

Mention of publicity is in order here. You hear sometimes: But do we really need all this wide criticism, self-criticism and publicity launched by the Central Committee? I shall tell you that we have only gained so far, losing nothing. The people have felt a surge of energy, they are bolder, more active at work and in public life. And, you know, all who tried to evade our laws now face the music. For there is nothing stronger than the force of public opinion when it can be realised. And it is only realised when there is criticism, self-criticism and broad publicity. We need publicity to accomplish the tasks set by the Congress, to get the people really involved in all the matters of state administration, a dream of Lenin.

By the way, many city and regional newspapers are conspicuously silent. National newspapers speak clear and loud, supporting everything positive and criticising the blunders and flaws, but not so the local newspapers. When a group of their editors was gathered in the Central Committee, they said plainly : "Well, you tell that to our city and district party committee secretaries." Indeed, why should the public not know about what is happening in the district or city? And judge that, speak out if need be. This is what socialism is all about, Comrades. Are newspaper editors present here? (A voice : Yes, there are).

I hope that city and district party committee secretaries will take this into account. They are in charge. It's their newspapers. You shouldn't fear publicity, Comrades. We are strong, the public is for socialism, for the policy of the party, for change, for readjustment. In general, the buildup of publicity by patchwork is intolerable. Publicity isn't a short-term campaign, but a norm of contemporary Soviet life, a constant, unbroken process in which some tasks are solved and new — usually, more difficult — tasks arise.

The same applies to criticism and self-criticism. If we do not subject ourselves to criticism and analysis, what will happen then? We have a direct need of this, vital need if the Party and society are to function normally.

We, Comrades, understand that very much now depends on our cadres, on the Party activists. Today most of these people hold the position they have won by their work, by their personal contribution to the country's cause. Enormous is their role as the organisers of people, as economic organisers, as the promoters of Party policy at this stage in Soviet society's development. Ambitious, highly interesting work has been undertaken in the nation.

I want to inform you that we have decided to devote the next Central Committee Plenum to cadre policy. Our line is as follows, Comrades: everything must develop according to the Leninist principles. We should have a combination of experienced and young cadres, through constant growth and promotion of personnel based on their political and professional qualities.

All our cadres, of course, need support. And this support will be forthcoming from the Central Committee and local Party committees. But it will combine with exactingness. I think this is a correct approach because trust presupposes, rather than excludes, high exactingness. Only in such an atmosphere will all the cadres act confidently and handle matters successfully. When there is such an atmosphere, it protects the people from errors; from possible blunders in their work. This is what we need. Therefore, we propose to discuss this question at the Central Committee Plenum in the light of the new tasks set by the Congress.

You, Comrades, have everything to conduct cadre policy more successfully, drawing on the experience amassed. Don't wait for the Plenum and its decisions, but, on the contrary, even in the pre-Plenum period, do much to raise the level of cadre work.

In conclusion, I want to say: I have benefited greatly from my communication with the working people, leaders and the Party activists in the Far East. I have had a frank, Party-spirited talk with many here, discussing the current situation and long-term goals, the real problems in the life of our society and the activity of the Party.

The Maritime and Khabarovsk territorial Party branches are big Party branches working in very important regions of our country. They are working for big targets right now, and still more significant targets will be tackled tomorrow.

Allow me, Comrades, to wish you great success in your undertakings, undertakings our people and society need, and to express the confidence that you will contribute what the Party expects from you.

(*Pravda,* August, 2, 1986)

APPENDIX — C

GUIDELINES FOR THE ECONOMIC AND SOCIAL DEVELOPMENT OF THE USSR FOR 1986-1990 AND FOR THE PERIOD ENDING IN 2000

For almost seven decades the Communist Party of the Soviet Union has been confidently leading the country along the road mapped out by the great Lenin. The 27th Congress of the CPSU will hold a special place in the heroic history of the Party and the people. Its task is to define the strategy of our Motherland's progress for an extremely important stage of communist construction and initiate a fundamental restructuring of all aspects of the life of Soviet society.

A detailed picture of the Party's and people's creative work has been given in the Political Report of the CPSU Central Committee to the 27th Congress by the General Secretary of the CPSU Central Committee Mikhail Gorbachev. Constructively, from the positions of the firm principles of Marxism-Leninism, it has profoundly substantiated the concept of accelerated socio-economic development, re-examined the entire range of problems related to the life of the Party, the state, and society. The Report has innovatively defined the strategy and tactics for the comprehensive perfection of socialism, and the domestic and foreign policies of the CPSU and the Soviet Government. On the basis of a deep class analysis it shows the correlation of forces in the modern world and the main trends and contradictions of its development and demonstrates the growing potential of the world socialist system. It has forcefully enunciated our stand on a question that worries humanity — the question of war and peace, of averting the nuclear threat.

*Report by Nikolai Ryzhkov, Chairman of the Council of Ministers of the USSR, to the 27th Congress of the CPSU — March 3, 1986.

The depth of the ideological content, creative thinking, and uncompromising attitude in assessing the causes of the shortcomings and difficulties that have piled up, and the realism and courage in formulating new tasks are grounds for regarding the Political Report of the CPSU Central Committee as a document of immense historic significance.

The moral and political climate that has taken shape under the impact of the CPSU Central Committee Plenary Meeting of April 1985, and the unwavering belief in the correctness of the course steered by the Party which permeates the Political Report have determined the whole atmosphere of the work of this Congress. It is proceeding in a businesslike manner, constructively, in an exacting spirit, and with a sense of the Party's high responsibility to the Soviet people. The discussion of the Political Report of the CPSU Central Committee and the new edition of the Party Programme convincingly demonstrates the monolithic unity of the Party ranks, the unity of thought, and the unity of action of the Soviet Communists, in fact of all the Soviet people.

The draft Guidelines for the Economic and Social Development of the USSR for 1986-1990 and for the Period Ending in 2000 is an important political and economic document submitted by the Party Central Committee for consideration by the Congress. Its pivot is the concept of acceleration advanced by the April Plenary Meeting of the CPSU Central Committee. The draft specifies the programme tasks and aims that will have to be attained before the end of the present century, and defines the principal directions for a qualitative transformation of the productive forces and of society's social development.

The draft Guidelines are entirely consonant with the vital interests of Soviet people, with their hopes for the future. This was shown with the utmost clarity by the truly countrywide discussion of the draft in which approximately 110 million citizens took part.

The entire discussion has further demonstrated the heightened political maturity of the working people, and the deep commitment of all strata of our society to reinforcing the might of the socialist Motherland.

The draft Guidelines have aroused considerable interest

abroad. There are, of course, dissimilarities in the attitude to it. Our class adversaries and foes are endeavouring to misrepresent the significance and aims of the outlined plans. But of course they cannot but acknowledge their scale and boldness. Our friends, in the fraternal socialist countries above all, see this document as graphic proof of the new social system's advantages, of its ability to solve the basic socio-economic problems of the day. With this they link the strengthening of our community and the consolidation of the positions of socialism, of all the progressive forces, and of the cause of peace in the world.

Economic and Social Development of the USSR during the 11th Five-Year Plan Period: Results and Conclusions

The Communist Party, which is steadfastly abiding by the Leninist traditions, combines, as it has always done, a broad view of the perspective with a realistic assessment of the state of the economy and potentialities for its further growth, with an objective analysis of the progress that has been made.

The draft Guidelines sum up the advances that have been made in the past five years. These give full grounds for drawing the conclusion that by their work the Soviet people have made a considerable contribution to advancing the country's economic might. This was the basis for the rise of the people's welfare and for the keeping of our country's defence capability at the proper level.

However, as you all know, work on the tasks charted by the 26th Congress proceeded in a situation that was not simple, while at the early stage, it may be said, the situation was extremely complex. The unfavourable tendencies that had appeared in the economic development in the 1970s grew sharper in the early 1980s rather than slackened. And this had an adverse effect on the fulfilment of the 11th Five-Year Plan. The slowdown of the growth rates continued during the first two years. The qualitative indicators of economic management lowered.

In 1982 the growth of industrial output was 1.5 times below the average of the 10th Five-Year Plan. This mounting of difficulties could not but influence the solution of important problems in the social sphere as well. For instance, in the second year of that Five-Year period the rise of the population's real incomes came virtually to a halt.

This was due to a number of factors. As for the fundamental causes of the shortcomings, they consist in the following: in practical work timely account was not taken of the changed economic situation mainly due to the exhaustion of the potentialities for extensive growth, and no proper perseverance was displayed in using the achievements of scientific and technological progress, and in restructuring the economy and its management system in accordance with the imperatives of the day. Besides, both in the centre and in the localities many leaders continued to apply outdated methods and proved unprepared for work in the new conditions. Discipline and order deteriorated impermissibly. There was a lowering of exactingness and responsibility. The vicious practice of the downward revision of plans became widespread. During these years there was a departure from the immutable principle of the socialist economy, for which the fulfilment of the plan is the law and norm of economic life. These phenomena were not given a principled political assessment and no practical conclusions were drawn.

After critically analysing the situation, the Party took steps to reinforce the management of economic development, chiefly in improving organisation and labour discipline. These steps were supported by the whole people and gave a certain impulse to our progress. As a result, from 1983, positive changes were noticeable, and this somewhat improved the situation with the fulfilment of the 11th Five-Year Plan.

During the Five-Year Plan period the national income rose 17 per cent and industrial output 20 per cent. The gas industry grew rapidly. In the volume of gas output the country now holds first place in the world. The output of electric energy from nuclear power stations more than doubled. The output of individual products of the engineering industry grew at priority rates. Some changes took place also in the building industry. Major steps were taken to carry out the Food Programme and this increased the volume of

	Total for 1981-1985, billion roubles	Absolute growth for 1981-1985 as against 1976-1980, billion roubles	Growth of total volume in 1981-1985 as against 1976-1980, per cent
National income, share used for consumption and accumulation	2,398	353	117
Industrial output	3,778	628	120
Agricultural output (in 1983 prices)	1,010	53	106
Freight turnover of all modes of transport (trillion ton-kilometres)	37.1	5.7	118
Installed basic assets	815	147	122
Capital investment	842	125	117
Retail trade turnover	1,466	226	118

agricultural output. In the latter half of the Five-Year period there were signs that the efficiency indicators of social production were improving.

It should be stressed that despite all the difficulties, the Party made the maximum effort to achieve the plan targets for the growth of the living standard advanced by the 26th Congress. There was a rise in the average monthly pay of factory and office workers and in the remuneration of collective farmers, and the social consumption funds were increased.

There was an improvement in pension schemes, in the system of health care, and a marked growth of state aid to families with children. Considerable funds were allocated for education and a school reform. As in previous Five-Year periods housing construction proceeded on a large scale. Over 10 million flats were turned over for tenancy. In conformity with directives from the Party, the process of the social restructuring of the countryside and the levelling up of the living standards of rural and urban dwellers continued.

Quite a lot was thus done during the Five-Year period. But we must give an objective assessment of its results and in a

	Guidelines targets approved by the 26th Congress	Actual fulfilment
Average monthly wages of factory and office workers, 1985 in per cent of 1980	113-116	113
Average monthly payment for the work of collective farmers, 1985 in per cent of 1980	120-122	129
Social consumption funds, 1985 in per cent of 1980	120	125
Housing completed in 1981-1985, million square metres overall	530-540	552
Pre-school facilities completed in 1981-1985, million places	2.5	2.9
Completed general schools in 1981-1985, million places	4.3	5.2
Hospital beds, 1985 in per cent of 1980	108-110	108.7
Specialists trained by institutions of higher learning and specialised secondary schools in 1981-1985, million	10	10.5

committed, Party spirit bring to light serious shortcomings that slow down our progress in order to draw the necessary conclusions for the future.

It must be stated frankly that the assignments of the five-Year Plan were not fully fulfilled. Many industries were unable to reach the planned targets. As a whole, during the Five-Year period there was an output shortfall of 35 million tons of finished rolled stock, 145 million tons of coal, over 50 million tons of oil, and consumer goods worth 16 billion roubles. The design, technical level, and quality of machines and equipment did not in all cases meet the requirements of the national economy. There was a systematic lag in the chemical and in the timber and woodworking industries. The principal general construction ministries failed to cope with their plans year after year. We did not receive the expected returns from the large resources invested in agriculture. The assignments for raising efficiency were regularly underfulfilled and scientific and technological progress was retarded.

All this affected the end results and proportions of economic development and incurred the loss of billions of roubles in the national income. One result of this was the nonfulfilment of a number of assignments for promoting the standard of living, including real incomes and the retail trade turnover. Complications arose in the state of finances and of money circulation.

The burden of the shortcomings that had been piling up over a long period was so great that it proved impossible to eliminate it within a short span of time. The individual steps that were taken could not halt the negative tendencies in the economy, direct the economy onto the path of stable and dynamic growth. This called for radical changes, a profound restructuring, and the Party was looking perseveringly for cardinal solutions of the problems confronting the country. It was precisely on this restructuring that the Communists and the Soviet people were orientated by the April 1985 Plenary Meeting of the CPSU Central Committee, which marked a turning point in the life of our society. It is this restructuring that meets pressing requirements and the Party's line for accelerating socio-economic development.

Our national economy has all the prerequisites for this: a powerful production, scientific, technological, and intellectual potential, skilled personnel, and natural resources. The main thing now is to use the advantages and growing possibilities of the planned socialist system and steadfastly implement the CPSU's economic strategy.

Acceleration of the Country's Social and Economic Development — A Strategic Task for the Period Ending in 2000

In the draft Guidelines the Party's course towards accelerating the country's socio-economic development for the period ending in 2000, taking Soviet society to a qualitatively new level, profoundly transforming its productive forces, and improving the relations of production is materialised in concrete assignments and figures.

The choice of a 15-year period was made, in the first place, on account of the increased magnitude and complexity of the tasks confronting the country, tasks that require more than one or two Five-Year periods to be carried out. Moreover, this is the optimal period in which the major breakthroughs of the present stage of the scientific and technological revolution, considering the forecasts for its development, can be used to their full extent.

Underlying the draft Guidelines is a scientific analysis of the ways and means of resolving major problems and carrying out comprehensive special-purpose programmes that will, in the main, embrace the period up to the year 2000: the Food and Energy programmes, the promotion of the engineering industry and the chemicalisation of the national economy, the development of the production of consumer goods and of the services industry. A 15-year period is thus realistically foreseeable and rests on a carefully tested foundation.

The economic targets that must be attained by the close of the twentieth century are defined entirely in keeping with the provisions of the new edition of the CPSU Programme. It is planned to double the national income and industrial output. There will be a substantial increase and radical transformation of the country's production apparatus. As a result, the economic potential that will be created in the course of 15 years will approximately equal that what has been built throughout all the preceding years of Soviet power, and a long stride forward will be taken in furthering the material and technical basis of communism.

Under socialism the principal purpose of social production is to maintain a continuous rise in the people's living standard and cultural level. At the present stage the Communist Party sets the task of placing the people's well-being on a higher, qualitatively new level.

Priority significance is attached to the solution of social problems in the sphere of labour, which is the main sphere of human activity. A prime task here is to reduce arduous and monotonous work. The share of manual work will fall by more than a half. This will allow releasing over 20 million people from unskilled work and make their labour meaningful and satisfying.

Provision is being made for radically resolving within the next 15 years pressing problems of material well-being and intellectual development, which are of particularly vital importance to all strata of society. In the first place, this means meeting in full the growing effective demand for high-quality and diverse goods and services, and reaching the rational norms of food intake recommended by science. A task of great social significance, that of providing practically every Soviet family with separate housing — flats or cottages — has to be carried out by the year 2000. This will require the utmost mobilisation of strength and funds, and continuous concern for this vital issue both at the centre and locally.

The system of education, personnel training, and medical services are to be improved radically, and the material facilities for culture, recreation, and sport, for the entire social sphere, are to be expanded considerably.

Of course, these targets of social production and the standard of living can be attained within the set time-limits only through a visible enhancement of the efficiency and speed of our advance.

Growth rates have always been and remain a central question in the Party's economic policy. Today, in the light of the concept of accelerating the country's socio-economic development this acquires a fundamental significance and a new content.

First, provision is made for giving the national income a more dynamic character. Its increment rate is to rise from an annual average of 3.1 per cent in the past Five-Year period to 5 per cent in the 14th Five-Year period. The negative tendency towards a slowdown of growth rates during the past three Five-Year periods will thereby be halted. The increment of the national income in absolute terms is to be even larger. As a result the national income to be produced in that period will total roughly 12 trillion roubles, which is more than the total for all the preceding years of Soviet power. This rise of the growth rates of the national income and of its increments in absolute terms is vital in order to carry out large-scale economic and social tasks simultaneously. Moreover, this is necessary for keeping the country's defence capability at the proper level.

Second, in the process of acceleration a more balanced structure of production is to be formed that will meet more comprehensively the growing and changing social requirements. This means that every percentage point of growth and every rouble must signify qualitatively new and effective products with high consumer properties, products needed by the national economy and the population. In this lies the immutable imperative of the present economic growth strategy.

Third and, I would say, it is most important that higher growth rates must be achieved on a fundamentally new basis, on the basis of comprehensive and consistent intensification. Setting this task, the Party indicates the principal means for carrying it out — a cardinal acceleration of scientific and technological progress and the attainment of the highest levels by science and technology. This is the catalyst of our progress, the operation of which will mount from one Five-Year plan period to another.

The Party approaches the intensification question comprehensively and broadly. Our economy has reached a level at which it can develop rapidly not through a steady growth of resources, as was formerly the case, but through comprehensive intensification of production, through intensification in all spheres. It is planned not only to boost labour productivity but also to reduce the material input per unit of production and the output-to-asset ratio, to transfer not only individual industries but the whole national economy onto the lines of intensification. This is the only sure way of accelerating economic and social development.

Raising the productivity of social labour is, in the long run, the trunk direction for solving socialism's basic problems. The decisive step in carrying out the programme task bequeathed to us by Lenin, namely, to reach the highest world level, will be taken within the next 15 years. The Guidelines provide for increasing labour productivity in the entire national economy 2.3-2.5-fold by the year 2000. As a result, the Soviet economy will enter upon a qualitatively new road of development: the growth of production will for the first time be ensured in parallel with a reduction of the need for manpower resources, and greater possibilities than ever before will be opened thereby for the solution of many social problems. All this will allow the pattern for distributing manpower resources to be formed more rationally to suit the more dynamic character of the national economy and, at the same time, will ensure full and effective employment. All that stems from the character and essence of the socialist social system.

The document we are considering contains a fundamentally new approach to meeting the economy's need for material resources. Whereas in preceding years this need was covered mainly by increasing production, now the long term task is to obtain 75-80 per cent of the growth rate of the needed fuel, energy, raw materials, metal, and other materials by economising these materials. The following example gives an idea of how effective this line is for the national economy. If the character of economic growth were to remain unchanged, by the end of the century we would need roughly 50 million tons more rolled stock than is currently planned. Realisation of the course towards saving resources will allow for a marked decrease of power-intensity and material input per unit of production.

The intensive growth and technical improvement of the production apparatus make particularly high demands of the output-to-asset ratio. Regrettably, the negative trend towards the decrease of this ratio has still not been overcome. In the coming 15 years it is planned to secure a breakthrough in the dynamics of this indicator as well: at the first stage — in the first half of the 1990s — to stabilise the output-to-asset ratio, and then ensure its growth.

New retooling of the national economy on the basis of the achievements of the scientific and technological revolution is a task of truly historic significance. Only in this case will comprehensive intensification rest on a solid foundation. This means rapid renewal and a qualitative improvement of the country's material and technical basis. It is very important that its high level is steadfastly maintained and that it conforms to world achievements. This process must embrace all industries. Every ministry and every industrial facility must have a concrete programme ensuring the steady renewal of productive assets and must carry it out perseveringly. This is vital for the solution not only of economic but also important social problems.

Such are the aims and main tasks for the development of the economy and the promotion of the people's living standard that the Party is setting for the long term. They are indeed impressive. Their fulfilment will significantly move the country along the road of social progress and considerably reinforce its economic positions in the world, enhancing the appeal of socialism. To carry out what has been planned will mean mobilising all our efforts and potentialities, bringing into operation the factors assisting the growth of socialist production, and promoting its efficiency.

And the main thing here is to secure the all-out vitalisation of the human factor. It is only by working and working effectively that we can carry out our plans and make them accomplished deeds. That is what the crucial political task is for every working person to take the programme objectives of the Party close to heart, to see them as his vital cause working in his interests and those of all society. That is the dependable earnest of our country's prosperity and of new successes in building communism.

The depth and dimension of the charted readjustments will necessitate raising the management of the national economy to a new, higher level. All industries and republics must have clear-cut orientations for the next 15 years. It is only in this way that we can clearly plan out the phases of our growth and ensure the continuity of aims and tactics of economic management in the period up to the close of the present century, and define the place and role of every Five-Year Plan in implementing the Party's economic strategy.

12th Five-Year Plan Period — A Crucial Stage in the Realisation of the Party's Economic Strategy

The 12th Five-Year Plan is a primary and extremely important stage in the practical implementation of the Party's long-term economic strategy. During these years there must be a marked growth of our economy and it must be taken to a higher trajectory of development, the trajectory of acceleration.

The main task of the Five-Year Plan has been defined from these positions. It consists in enhancing the growth rates and eficiency of economic development through accelerated scientific and technological progress, the retooling and technical reconstruction of industry, the intensive utilisation of the existing production potential, an improvement of the economic management system, of the economic mechanism, and the attainment, on this basis, of a further rise in the Soviet people's living standard.

Permit me to report to you, comrade delegates, that the indicators for the growth and efficiency of social production envisaged in the draft Guidelines fully ensure the attainment of the main aim of the 12th Five-Year Plan.

The dynamic character of the national economy is strikingly and convincingly reflected in the growing absolute increments of key economic indicators. The increment in the national income will increase 60 per cent in 1986-1990. It must be noted that there was a fall in this indicator during the past five years.

As a result, in 1990 the national income will reach 614 billion roubles and the volume of industrial output will rise to one trillion roubles. These are the rates and dimensions that will characterise our economy by the beginning of the last decade of the twentieth century.

The 12th Five-Year Plan will have yet another hallmark. Its purpose is to lay the foundation for the rise in the growth rate of the country's socio-economic development in the subsequent ten years. When determining economic proportions it was mandatory to pay special attention to investment policy. During the preceding three Five-Year Plan periods there was a steady and substantial fall in the growth rates of capital investments, and which could not but retard the renewal of fixed assets, the expansion of capacities and, in the final count, the economic development as a whole.

Proceeding from the course of acceleration, the CPSU Central Committee saw the expediency of increasing the

	Increment in absolute terms, billion roubles		Average annual growth rate, per cent	
	1985 against 1980	1990 against 1985 envisaged in the draft Guidelines	11th Five-Year Plan	12th Five-Year Plan envisaged in the draft Guidelines
National income used for consumption and accumulation	71	96-111	3.1	3.5-4.0
Industrial output	135	169-194	3.7	3.9-4.4
of which means of production (group A)	99	123-142	3.6	3.7-4.2
consumer goods (group B)	36	46-52	3.9	4.1-4.6
Agricultural output (average annual output growth against the preceding Five-Year Plan, in prices for 1983)	11	28-32	1.1	2.7-3.0
Retail trade turnover	46	59-73	3.1	3.4-4.0
Volume of paid services to the population	9.8	13.7-18.2	5.0	5.4-7.0

growth rate of investments in production under the 12th Five-Year Plan up to 25 per cent as against 16 per cent in the past five years. Naturally, this means certain changes in the pattern of the distribution of the national income such as increasing the share of the accumulation fund. This manoeuvre is necessary in order to attain both current and long-term aims. The share of accumulation will subsequently be stabilised and even somewhat reduced.

This manoeuvre, it must be emphasised, will be carried out under conditions of enhanced efficiency of social production, which will allow a significant increase in the absolute size of the consumption fund determining the Soviet people's standard of living. I will give you some statistics. The increment in the consumption fund during the 12th Five-Year Plan period will amount to 74 billion roubles compared with 55 billion roubles during the past five years. The real incomes of the population will grow faster. This character of development is entirely in keeping with the Party's long-term course for the intensification of the social orientation of our plans.

During the 12th Five-Year Plan period a decisive step is to be made in carrying out an urgent economic and political task, that of the national economy's transition to intensive development. The growth of end results will take place in conditions of substantial reductions in the increments of basic resources and simultaneous improvements in the qualitative indicators of work.

	Increment for five years (per cent)		Growth (+), fall (–) of increment rates
	1981-1985	1986-1990 as envisaged in draft Guidelines	
I. Results of Production			
National income share used for consumption and accumulation	17	19-22	+2 to 5
Industrial output	20	21-24	+1 to 4
Agricultural output (average annual)	6	14-16	+8 to 10
II. Basic Resources			
Number of people employed in material production	2.3	0.5	–1.8
Fixed production assets	37	30	–7
Production of instruments of labour	17	15	–2

The Guidelines envisage increasing the productivity of social labour 20-23 per cent as against 16.5 per cent in the past Five-Year Plan period. For the first time ever it is planned to obtain practically the entire increment in the national income and in the output of industry and other branches of material production through higher labour productivity. This is one of the fundamental features of the new

Five-Year Plan. The growth rate of manpower resources during these years will fall and amount to only 3,200,000 persons. Without the planned growth of labour productivity the national economy would require an additional workforce of more than 22 million. We simply do not have such manpower resources. In the 12th Five-Year Plan period it seems possible not only to get by with the existing increment but direct almost all of it into education, health care, and other social and cultural spheres, whereas in the past Five-Year period the increment in manpower resources was distributed about equally between production and non-production spheres.

In conformity with the course worked out by the Party it is planned to substantially accelerate the fulfilment of an important task such as making the economy the main source for satisfying the additional requirements in fuel and in raw and other materials. It is planned that this source will in the next five years cover 60-65 per cent of the growth of the demand for basic resources. As a result, in 1990 the saving of material resources will double in the national economy as a whole. Resource-saving on this scale is unprecedented in our country. It reflects the objective needs of the present stage of our development.

The ways of resolving the resource-saving problem are diverse. First of all, this means broad use of the latest equipment and technology, of up-to-date forms of organisation, and an effective economic mechanism. And, certainly, such material conditions and such a moral and ethical climate in every work collective in which all working people, all Soviet people, will become the motivated and active participants in this major undertaking.

Another important direction is the maximum utilisation of recycled resources. Their share in industrial consumption is still not large enough, although a great deal of positive experience has been accumulated in some republics. In this the Ukrainian SSR is a good example. There are tangible achievements in this sphere also in fraternal socialist countries. In the future it is planned to substantially increase the share of recycled raw materials to an average of at least 10-12 per cent. The heads of ministries and leaders of Union republics must fundamentally change their attitude to this matter. Often, speaking figuratively, they sit on huge wealth and, at the same time, complain of having a shortage of raw materials. Moreover, one should also be mindful of the huge damage that is being done to the environment. The utilisation of recycled resources must be approached by the State Planning Committee of the USSR and the State Supplies Committee of the USSR from principled, state positions.

Among the major tasks involved in raising efficiency, that of the quality of output and of work is the most acute and urgent. This is not only an economic but also a political problem. Within a short span of time we have advanced to the front-rank positions in the world in the output of many products. We now can and are obliged to resolve the problem of quality with undiminished perseverance. The national economy has reached a point where not a single important production or social problem can be solved without a radical improvement of the state of affairs as regards output quality.

The improvement of the quality of output is, in the final analysis, also a question of its quantity, of saving resources, and of more fully satisfying society's needs. I'll give just one example. It is well known how acute the question of tyres is in the country. This is known also by the Ministry of the Petrochemical Industry. The most rational way of resolving this problem is to increase the life-span of tyres. To raise this indicator by 10 per cent would be tantamount to producing six million tyres annually. This is practically the amount we need today to meet the demands of the national economy and of the population. Many such examples can be given.

The draft Guidelines envisage an approximate doubling of the proportion of top-quality industrial products in the next five years. At the same time, it is necessary to substantially enhance the role and objectivity of certification. A pressing issue of today is the effective utilisation of the economic mechanism that imposes material and moral penalties on enterprises which manufacture low-quality products. Conversely, work collectives that produce up-to-date high-quality products, and we have quite a few of such collectives, should be encouraged, and the encouragement should be generous. Important decisions have now been adopted: substantial pay hikes and rigid sanctions have been introduced. Enterprises and associations should rapidly restructure their work so that the new demands on qualiity do not catch anybody unawares.

The improvement of quality is a nation-wide task and it can only be carried out by the combined efforts of managerial bodies at all levles, all enterprises, and all working people relying on the achievements of modern science and technology and on the initiative and creativity of the masses. Every factor must be brought into play: economic, administrative, and educational. Nor can half-measures be tolerated in this matter. What is needed is the utmost mobilisation of forces, perseverance, and consistency in fulfilling the adopted decisions. This is how the question of quality is put in the letter of the CPSU Central Committee to all the working people. And this is the way it must be resolved.

Comrades, the draft Guidelines have set highly important and high pressure assignments for the growth of output and for the improvement of the people's well-being. During these years it is envisaged to provide the Soviet Armed Forces with everything they need to defend our Motherland. The 12th Five-Year Plan, which gives the start to the Party's long term strategy, must become a turning point for our economy in all respects — from the point of view of growth rates and that of efficiency. It must become a turning point, too, in the way of organising the fulfilment of the Five-Year Plan.

Conclusions must be drawn from the lessons of the past, when the focus in the fulfilment of Five-Year Plans was shifted to the closing years of the Five-Year period. A directive of the Central Committee of the CPSU envisages, already in 1986, the first year of the current Five-Year Plan, such rates for the development of the national economy that would allow a more even distribution of the assignments of the Five-Year Plan, thereby providing real conditions for its fulfilment. All this requires high pressure work from the very start of the Five-Year period and sets the necessary rhythm for the subsequent years.

No time should be lost in mobilising available organisational and social resources, and key, long-term factors of acceleration, and scientific and technological progress in the first place, should be set in motion. It is only by linking up all these areas of work that we shall carry out our plans and achieve the set social targets.

Lines of Economic Intensification in the 12th Five-Year Plan Period

1. Acceleration of Scientific and Technological Progress: Main Lever of Intensification

The Party's policy of all-round intensification rests on the enormous potential of the current stage of the scientific and technological revolution. Lenin's words that "in order to build communism we must take technology and science and make them available to wider circles," are now more relevant than ever before. Today, putting science and technology into action means accelerating scientific and technological progress in the top priority fields, ensuring rapid and large-scale application of everything that is progressive, and transforming the productive forces qualitatively. It also means joint development and effective utilization of scientific and technical achievements by the socialist community countries and active participation in the world-wide division of labour.

Our country has always paid special attention to the advancement of science and technology. In a brief span of time we have built up a powerful scientific potential which has enabled us, at each stage, to successfully carry out major economic and defence tasks. It is no secret, however, that although we possess noteworthy research and development results and advanced ideas we often lag behind in the introduction of progressive technologies, including even some that were developed in our country. This situation can only be explained by miscalculations made by ministries in their technological policy, and, at times, by their unwillingness to look ahead.

On the basis of an in-depth analysis the Plenary Meeting of the Central Committee of the CPSU in April 1985 and the June 1985 Conference of the Party's Central Committee seriously posed the question of energetically eliminating barriers in the way of scientific and technological progress, and of ensuring cardinal, revolutionary changes all along the line. The strategy which the Party has worked out for accelerating scientific and technological progress consists, first, in concentrating the available resources on the key avenues while advancing science and technology in all spheres. Second, in providing scope for the large-scale application of reliable technological innovations tested in practice, from which it is possible to obtain the maximum returns before they become morally obsolete. Third, in quickly and purposefully carrying out research and development that will lead to the development and introduction of fundamentally new equipment and production methods ensuring a manifold increase in productivity. The solution of these problems will be put on a practical footing in the 12th Five-Year Plan period.

Broad development of advanced technologies is one of the most important lines of scientific and technological progress. Only by taking this road will it be possible to bring about changes raising to a qualitatively new level not only individual lines of production but also entire industries. In the 12th Five-Year Plan period we intend to extend the use of progressive technologies basic to each industry by 50 to 100 per cent. Fundamentally new production methods, for instance, membrane, laser, plasma, superhigh pressures, pulse loads, etc., will hold a notable place. The scale on which these methods are applied will be increased several times over, and that will undoubtedly yield a big economic effect.

Another avenue is automation and mechanisation of production that will radically transform work places and make the job of workers, collective farmers and the intelligentsia more productive, creative and attractive. That is one of the principal social objectives that the Party has set itself. The level of automation in the national economy will double on the average. About 5,000 automated control systems are to be introduced in industry.

The present-day stage in automation is based on the revolution in computer technology, in computerisation of the national economy. New generations of computers of all classes, from supercomputers to personal computers for school instruction, are to be designed and introduced in the coming five years. Total output of computers is to go up by 2.3 times in the five years. We are setting the target of large-scale computerisation of the machinery and equipment produced for all industries. The future belongs to this technology.

A characteristic feature of automation in the 12th Five-Year Plan period is rapid expansion of robotics, rotor lines and rotor conveyers, and flexible automated production lines, which ensure high productivity. For example, the number of industrial robots is to be trebled during these five years.

As we see, the scale is sizable. A fundamentally new approach is necessary to the application of this advanced, and, it must be said, costly equipment. Yet at present it is being used extremely inefficiently by many ministries. Thus, according to data released by the USSR Committee of People's Control, at the plants of the Ministry of the Electrical Engineering Industry highly productive machining centres are not operating at full load, and some simply stand idle. At many enterprises of the Ministry of Agricultural Machinery and the Ministry of Power Engineering, digital control machine-tools are being used less than one shift per day. That style of work discredits the potentialities of the latest technology and does great damage to the economy. The situation must be remedied immediately.

It is intended to substantially reduce materials consumption in social production through the large-scale application of economical types of metal products, plastics, and other progressive materials. In the course of the five years their output is to increase by more than 30 per cent, as compared to an increase of only 6 per cent in the production of traditional materials. The application of fundamentally new construction materials which have been developed by our scientists and which are greatly superior in quality to those now being used opens up tremendous prospects. That refers, in particular, to composite materials. Their manufacture is to increase by 10-12 times in the 12th Five-Year Plan period.

The scale of introducing new machinery and technologies

outlined for the Five-Year period as a whole will ensure a more than 65 per cent growth in the productivity of social labour and will reduce production costs in industry by 28 billion roubles.

Rapid progress in science and technology calls for a continuous and growing renewal of scientific ideas and developments. The decisive role here is played by fundamental research, by the Academy of Scienes of the USSR, which has splendid traditions and outstanding achievements. College and university research can also do a good deal. However, its discoveries will benefit the national economy only if they are taken up and applied in good time, that is, if all levels of the science-production cycle function smoothly and rhythmically.

Sectoral science economy is a highly important element of this chain. It possesses a ramified network of research institutes and design bureaus having a large number of researchers, and good results are obtained wherever they are competently used. That is not the case everywhere, however. All too often, sectoral organisations have been marking time, producing no tangible results. At times their efforts are subordinated to upholding narrow departmental interests, they lack a creative spirit and are distinguished by petty projects and by fragmentation of resources and personnel. Although they are aware of this, the heads of many ministries take an inert, irresponsible attitude to making use of the enormous scientific and technological potential. On the other hand, they display enviable activity in purchasing abroad machinery and technologies which they themselves could have successfully developed. This harmful practice must be subjected to severe and principled Party criticism.

The unbridled chase for imported technology and production techniques on the part of many a manager has a corrupting effect on designers. Seeing how easily equipment can be bought abroad, their ardour tends to dampen, they lose their zeal and bow to difficulties. Far be it from us to renounce using the results of the international division of labour and exchange of scientific and technical knowledge, but we must first and foremost rely on our own enormous scientific potential. In the new Five-Year Plan period we must energetically reorganise sectoral scientific research, bring it as close to production as possible, improve its material base, especially pilot plant and experimental facilities, and supply it with up-to-date instruments and research equipment. It must bear full responsibility for the scientific and technological level of its industry. That should be the main criterion in assessing its performance.

Special attention must be paid to scientific research at factory level. It stands closest of all to production, interlocks with it, and, as experience shows, significantly reduces the time needed to develop and produce new machinery. The Elektrosila, Uralmash, Ivanovo machine-tool production association, and other associations largely owe their fame to factory scientists, designers, and technologists. This sphere of research should be expanded at the fastest rates, and sectoral research institutes should be boldly integrated with it. We must speed up the organising of research-and-production associations to accelerate scientific and technological progress. This process has already begun in the engineering industry and must be actively taken up in other industries.

On the basis of the experience of leading research organisations inter-sectoral scientific and technical complexes have been arising lately. They straddle the main avenues of scientific and technological progress and are a new effective way of combining research with production.

The main thing, of course, is to provide the economic, social, and organisational prerequisites for creative work by engineers, scientists, and designers. They are the ones who generate scientific ideas and developments, and it is on them, first and foremost, that the technical level of production depends. A number of major decisions have been passed to stimulate their activity, to enhance their social prestige and to provide them with more incentives.

New forms of payment are to be introduced, which have proved their worth, overcome levelling trends, and encourage work that yields a high level of creative results. There was a time when many executives insisted on introducing these forms of payment. It is therefore hard to explain the fact that today these new forms have been introduced in less than a dozen enterprises and associations. All this shows how great is inertia in matters of scientific and technological progress and how much energetic, large-scale actions are needed.

We will have to resolutely restructure the economic mechanism in order to accelerate scientific and technological progress in every sector of the economy. But we must remember that this mechanism will yield no results by itself if the responsibility of the top managers, first of all the ministers, is not heightened at the same time. They must bear full responsibility for the technical standard of production in their industries.

In tackling the new tasks related to scientific and technical policy, a good deal depends upon the USSR State Committee for Science and Technology which has not yet found its place in the process, and has failed to readjust to the needs of the times. It should concentrate on coordinating the main lines of scientific and technological progress, on carrying out direct guidance of the inter-sectoral scientific and technical complexes and on organising scientific information in the country. It also has the highly important function, new for it, of coordinating efforts to carry out the Comprehensive Programme for Scientific and Technological Progress of the CMEA Member-Countries up to the Year 2000. Finally, the entire system of management of scientific and technological progress must be radically reorganised if we want to make it an inseparable element of our plans and of our entire economic life. This refers to the practice of planning, to the financing, price formation and incentive systems and to the entire economic mechanism.

In a world, comrades, a first-priority task of the 12th Five-Year Plan is that every engineering and managerial decision should be examined in the context of the gradually growing contribution by science and technology to production. Socialism's economic system enables us to make systematic use of the potential of the scientific and technological revolution. Unlike capitalism, where, in the final analysis, the great achievements of science and technology aggravate the social contradictions, in the hands of the socialist state they are a powerful lever for transforming society. Here socialism has a historic advantage, and must use it to the full.

2. *Investment Policy and Capital Construction*

An active investment policy is an effective instrument in implementing the Party's economic strategy. It is subordinated, in each particular period, to solving the main tasks confronting our country. The new feature of the investment policy in the 12th Five-Year Plan is its orientation on accelerating scientific and technological progress and, on this basis, qualitatively transforming the material base and structure of production.

The increase in capital investments is to be substantially greater in the current Five-Year Plan period: by up to 170 billion roubles, as compared to 125 billion roubles in 1981-1985. Total capital investments are to reach nearly one trillion roubles.

It is not only a matter, of course, of enormous capital investments. The success of an investment policy is determined largely by how effectively the resources are used, by how their sectoral and reproduction structure is shaped, and by how the very process of capital construction is organised. All these aspects have been thoroughly elaborated during the drafting of the Guidelines.

An important feature of the 12th Five-Year Plan is the considerable, 80 per cent, growth in capital investments in the engineering complex, the complex in which scientific and technological progress is embodied. Special emphasis is being put on developing its branches that provide for qualitative changes in the technological level of the engineering industry itself. That lays the material foundation for accelerating scientific and technological progress.

Among the key sectors, the fuel and energy complex gets special attention. Against the background of increasingly complicated extraction and transportation of fuel, capital investments in this sphere have to be increased 47 per cent to ensure reliable supplies of fuel for our country and for the other socialist community countries. Capital investment growth rates in the industries that ensure effective fuel extraction and refining methods will be approximately twice as high.

In conformity with the Food Programme a third of all

capital investments is being allocated to the agro-industrial complex. Here, priority goes to the sectors that process agricultural raw materials; capital investments in them will grow 51 per cent, as compared to the overall growth of 22 per cent. This will help to eliminate the big imbalance hindering growth of the final product.

A characteristic feature of the new Five-Year Plan is the emphasis it puts on retooling and modernising existing production facilities. The share of capital investments for these purposes is to grow from 37 per cent in 1985 to 50 per cent in 1990. This percentage will be still greater in the sectors and regions having the most outdated production facilities.

Revision of the reproductive structure of capital investments will considerably speed production apparatus renewal, overcoming the trend towards its physical and moral obsolescence which has taken shape lately. The average annual coefficient for scrapping outdated equipment is to increase to between 5 and 6 per cent, that is, to a level ensuring the planned production efficiency of the economy. Such a scale of renewal provides the possibility of substantially reducing the outlays for major overhauls. It is clear that considerable changes will also have to be made in the depreciation policy to solve these problems.

As the economic sectors go over to the new economic mechanism, the main role in technical retooling and reconstruction will be played by the development funds of enterprises and associations earned by their respective work collectives. And that calls for a radical change in the attitude to these funds. People at the enterprises must be fully informed of the fact that the main source of their technical retooling will be the first to receive all requisite resources. A special responsibility devolves here on the central economic agencies and, of course, the ministries, which, however, are continuing to operate in the old way with regard to this issue. The matter was rightly raised in the speeches at the Congress.

The priority given to retooling and modernisation will demand a certain cutback in the number of new projects, especially in the European part of our country. New projects will be carried out only for the purpose of major structural changes, of establishing industries that have arisen in the present stage of the scientific and technological revolution, and also of developing natural riches. Our fundamental policy consists in extensive retooling plus whatever new construction is vitally necessary.

A radical reorganisation of capital construction to make it more efficient is the keystone of the investment policy. Many unresolved problems have accumulated in this sphere over the years. Construction time-limits have been grossly violated, construction projects have become more expensive and the percentage of unfinished construction projects and stocks of uninstalled equipment has grown excessively. A completely abnormal situation has arisen in which the unsatisfactory work of building organisations, and the weakness of their industrial facilities have, in some regions, limited economic development and dealt tangible damage to the rational distribution of productive forces. The state of affairs in the building industry was doubtless affected by the general decline in discipline and responsibility witnessed in the past few years.

The problems of capital construction must be tackled without delay by using all the economic and organisational measures. A number of decisions aimed at improving the state of affairs in this industry have been adopted lately. Their strict fulfilment should yield the required results in the years immediately ahead. It is obvious, however, that the work will not end at that.

First and foremost, we must clamp down on the fragmentation of financial resources. Although we have been talking about this a long time, more than 300,000 large and small construction projects are underway throughout the country. That is an impermissible number, even taking our enormous size into account. The Central Committee of the CPSU has obliged us to normalise the situation. Beginning from 1987 we intend to go over to strict observance of standard time-limits in planning and carrying out construction work.

That is not a simple matter. Some might find it highly painful. We do not exclude the possibility that a number of projects not of primary importance will have to be shelved, and the manpower and funds reallocated. But we must take this step.

The front of construction work must be narrowed. In that case alone will we be able to really reduce building schedules by at least a half. Already today all the ministries and departments and the constituent republics must make thorough preparations for this work.

Implementation of the five-year investment programme calls for a higher level of industrialisation in capital construction. It must be put on a fundamentally new material and technical foundation. The old foundation, laid in the late fifties and early sixties, has largely exhausted its possibilities. The new foundation should rest on the latest achievements of science and technology at home and abroad and should contribute to the establishment of an integrated industrial construction process. The draft Guidelines provide for an increase in the number of projects built of prefabricated elements and in the delivery of mechanisms; the use of aluminium, plastics, and new materials is to increase 50 to 100 per cent. All this will substantially improve construction organisation, and raise labour productivity and construction standards while simultaneously reducing building costs. But a great deal still has to be done, and we shall return more than once to the question of industrialising capital construction.

It is equallly important to radically improve designing in the building industry. This is mostly a matter for the designers themselves, of course. The technical level of production, the more efficient use of capital investments and the intensification of construction depend to a large extent on them. They must be the catalysts of scientific and technological progress in all sectors of the economy.

We have splendid examples of new and modernised enterprises designed and built according to the latest word in technology. On the other hand, patently backward technical solutions as well as errors in project cost estimation often occur. In the four years of the last Five-Year Plan period the cost of construction projects went up by 11 billion roubles, or by 24 per cent of the initial estimates. Moreover, the technical and economic indices of half of the projects deteriorated. Herein lies the answer to the numerous requests to increase investment in production. Here lies an important source for solving many social problems.

The responsibility for the unsatisfactory situation in designing falls not only on the designers but also on the ministries and departments. They are the ones that give the go-ahead to outdated designs. According to the USSR Construction Bank (Stroibank), 25 per cent of the projects which are carried over into the 12th Five-Year Plan period and which are regarded by respective ministries as corresponding to the modern level of scientific and technological progress, were designed 10 to 20 years ago. This is a very alarming fact. It is quite understandable that such an approach cannot produce designs which measure up to modern demands. A situation of this kind is to be observed in many ministries. For example, the USSR Ministry of Non-Ferrous Metals has confirmed the high technical level of 69 projects that were approved between 1965 and 1975, while the Ministry of the Motor Vehicle Industry has confirmed 20. These construction projects would go into operation 20 or more years after they were designed. Need I make any comments?

The USSR State Committee for Construction (Gosstroi) is obliged to do much to improve the state of affairs in designing. While not taking over the duties of ministries and design organisations it should pursue a uniform scientific and technical policy in construction, draw up a system of assessments of the standards and technical level of designs, and widely practise design competitions.

Finally, a top-priority task is to reorganise construction management. This is perhaps the most neglected industry with regard to improving management and economic operation methods. Yet this question is more acute here than in any other sphere. Fragmentation and multi-level management must be eliminated and an optimal combination of centralisation with broader powers and greater responsibility of constituent republics and local bodies must be found.

Thus, capital construction must be improved at all levels. We must declare most definitely that the feasibility of our plans and the country's economic development rates depend largely on this.

3. *Structural Policy and the Growth of Economic Complexes*

At all stages in the development of the national economy our Party has attached exceptional importance to the structural policy, to the choice of priorities, to the drawing up of inter-sectoral and inner-sectoral proportions.

The draft Guidelines thoroughly define the most important assignments for improving the structure of the national economy and developing its sectors, and set forth the targets they have to reach. Allow me to dwell only on the most fundamental aspects of the structural policy in the 12th Five-Year Plan period.

First of all, it calls for priority growth of the end product — machines, equipment, consumer goods, completed construction projects — as compared with the intermediate product — fuel, raw materials and semi-manufactures. In 1986-1990, the increase in the end product per rouble of the increase in the value of raw and other materials will be 40 per cent greater than in the previous five-year period. The end product growth rate in the manufacturing industries will be 100 per cent higher than in the fuel and raw materials industries. This shift is based to a significant degree on the resource-saving policy.

Another feature is accelerated development of the industries — electric power, chemical, petrochemical and, of course, engineering — which will bring the national economy to the forefront of world science and technology. Their share in industry will amount to 41 per cent in 1990.

Finally, a very important feature is that all industries without exception have been oriented to a greater degree than before on the manufacture of consumer goods and the development of the service sphere. It is planned to give more priority to the growth of the B group industry than to the A group.

The most substantial structural changes are connected with greater priority for engineering. While the Guidelines were being drafted the Central Committee of the Party warned against underestimating the leading role of engineering and pointed to the need to overcome the previous trend towards bringing its growth rate close to that of industry as a whole. The growth rate of this sector under the 12th Five-Year Plan is 90 per cent higher than in industry as a whole. This is a very substantial coefficient and it will strengthen the priority position of engineering in the national economy.

The cardinal task of the machine-builders is to change the structure of production and to raise the qualitative specifications of machinery and equipment. By 1990 the annual renewal of engineering products is to be brought up to 13 per cent, as compared to 4.5 per cent in 1985. Against the background of the priority growth of engineering, this will provide a genuine foundation for retooling our country's production facilities on a modern basis.

Special attention is being paid to modernising the engineering industry. Its technical level depends primarily on the levels reached in machine tool-building, instrument-making, electronics and electrical engineering, which are therefore to grow much faster than the engineering industry as a whole. At the same time, each machine-building ministry must develop its own machine tool production geared to its industry's specific needs.

The tasks confronting machine-building have called for an improved management of this complicated sector. An Engineering Bureau under the USSR Council of Ministers has been set up and is putting its work in top gear.

Significant changes are planned in the structural materials complex. The main thing here is to increase the share of progressive, economical types of materials. Thanks to this, the national economy's growing demand for structural materials will be met by significantly lower output growth rates. That will be an important contribution by the complex to saving the country's resources.

For example, large-scale retooling in the iron and steel industry will improve the structure and quality of metal products. As a result, with a mere 9 per cent increase in the output of finished rolled products, industrial output as a whole will rise 21 to 24 per cent and engineering and metal-working will register a 40 to 45 per cent gain during the five-year period. Simultaneously, we must ensure a more rational use of metals, first and foremost, in engineering and construction.

In the non-ferrous metals industry the main stress is put on the comprehensive use of resources and on increasing the output of new types of goods. The replacement of metals and other traditional materials by chemical materials will be speeded up. Manufacture of the latest types of plastics is to increase nearly six-fold. Priority is also given to expanding the output of up-to-date timber products.

An equally important aspect of the development of this complex will be a better ratio between raw materials extraction and finished products. Thus, the output of ferrous metal rolled stock is to increase with hardly any growth in ore extraction or in pig iron and coke manufacture. The output of wood products per cubic metre of timber shipped out is to increase 16 per cent. All the above will be achieved by raising the technological level of these industries.

Reliable development of the entire national economy requires further improvement of the fuel and energy complex. Major shifts in the structure of the fuel-and-energy balance are to be carried out in conformity with the USSR Energy Programme. By the end of the five-year period nuclear power stations will nearly double their share of power production and will account for more than 20 per cent of the total amount generated.

In the course of the 11th Five-Year Plan period the USSR Ministry of the Power Industry fell short of its targets in starting up nuclear power plants, which created an additional demand for fossil fuels. Taking into account our country's strained fuel balance and the growing role of nuclear power generation, setbacks of this kind are impermissible in future.

The share of natural gas in the fuel and energy resources is to increase to 38 per cent. The gas industry is coping with its assignments not badly, but there are no grounds for complacency. After the Urengoi deposit reaches its designed capacity the increase in natural gas extraction will come chiefly from the Yamburg deposit. The main thing now is to speed up its development. A great amount of work has to be done to provide for the future.

The state of affairs in oil extraction, especially in Western Siberia, requires substantial improvement. By the end of the five-year period it should account for two-thirds of the Soviet

Union's total oil output. Failures in the work of this industry created difficulties for the economy. The Ministry of the Oil Industry, the Tyumen Chief Oil and Gas Administration and its enterprises turned out to be unprepared for operation when the output of wells at major deposits began to fall. The existing lag must be overcome in the shortest possible time. The Party and the Government have given the oilmen considerable assistance. Success now depends on the Ministry's organisational work, on its resolve to unfailingly carry out the assignments set forth in the Guidelines and mobilise the work collectives for achieving this. The local Party and economic bodies must play a big part in ensuring extraction of the planned volumes of oil.

In the coal industry, open-cast mining, especially in the Eastern regions, is getting special attention. Retooling and modernisation of the collieries in the old coal-mining areas, in the first place, in the Donetsk and Kuznetsk basins, should also be continued.

A dynamic development of the economy requires large-scale geological prospecting, especially for oil, natural gas, and ores, and higher efficiency and quality in preparing the explored mineral reserves for extraction.

A most important aspect of structural reorganisation is greater emphasis on the fuller satisfaction of the Soviet people's varied and ever-growing requirements. This is being achieved through accelerated development of the food-processing and non-food industries.

In the 12th Five-Year Plan period, closer and better-coordinated interaction among the branches within the agro-industrial complex will be achieved; this will ensure high end results of its work. Agriculture will develop considerably and its material and technical base will be consolidated. All types of farm output will grow thanks to the better provision of collective farms and state farms with new machinery, mineral fertilizers, chemical weed- and pest-killers, through increasing the area of improved land and making effective use of these resources. It is planned to bring the output of grain to 250-255 million tons and that of meat to 21 million tons. Such a good showing can only be made by using intensive technologies, increasing grain yields and livestock productivity, and by applying new methods of economic management within the agro-industrial complex. The coming five years will be highlighted by priority development of the processing industries and transportation, and better storage facilities for farm produce. All this will reduce unwarranted outlays and losses, enlarge the food resources and improve their quality.

The consumer goods output targets have been set according to the Comprehensive Programme for Developing Consumer Goods Production and Services, which open up broad vistas for their growth and improvement. The task is to bring the light and local industries, the services and trade to the frontlines of technological progress, and accelerate their development rates. It is planned to increase the manufacture of non-food goods by 30 per cent over the next five years, that is, to ensure a greater growth rate here than in industrial production as a whole. The range of goods will be considerably broadened and their quality improved.

The comprehensive and well-coordinated development of infrastructure — transport, communication and information system, material and technical supplies, warehousing and roads — is of increasing importance to our economy.

Transport workers face the responsible task of handling the ever-growing freight and passenger traffic, especially between the European and Eastern parts of the country. Its successful accomplishment calls for coordinated operation of all kinds of transport, development of new types of transport, and further consolidation of its material and technical base. To link all collective farm and state farm centres with the district administrative centres by motor roads in the 12th Five-Year Plan period is a task of tremendous industrial and social importance.

The approach to the development of all constituent republics and major regions is formulated in the national interest of the rational territorial division of social labour within the national economic complex. The targets in the draft Guidelines have been set in such a way as to further the economic and cultural development of all republics and to ensure a better location of the productive forces. Each republic should make a weighty contribution to building up the country's economic potential.

One of the most important territorial problems is to provide a closer linkage between industrial siting and the available manpower and material resources. As known, the resources of various kinds are unevenly distributed over our country's territory. The larger part of the production assets is concentrated in the European regions of the USSR, while fuel and raw materials production is being predominantly developed in Siberia. At the same time, the highest rate of growth of manpower resources is registered in Central Asia and the Transcaucasian area. The draft Guidelines provide for the siting of energy-intensive industries close to fuel and energy producers and for increasing the number of work places in regions having the requisite manpower resources. They pay special attention to the comprehensive economic development of Siberia and the Soviet Far East, to the exploitation of their natural riches and the provision of transport links with them.

Intensification and scientific and technological progress are thus the keynotes of the structural policy in the 12th Five-Year Plan period. This policy provides a solid foundation for strengthening the national economy's material and technical base.

4. Improvement of the System of Administration and Management Methods

Comrades, the success of our plans and objectives is indissolubly linked with the improvement of administration and methods of economic management. We will not be able to place production on the path of all-round intensification using the previous methods and old organisational forms, without changing them radically to suit the new conditions and present-day requirements for economic growth. What we want here are not partial improvements but, as Mikhail Gorbachev said in the Political Report, a radical reform.

To speak plainly, the insistent need for improving the system of administration was in many ways underestimated until recently. The job was being done slowly and half-heartedly. The bias for old, mainly administrative methods kept taking the upper hand and acted as a brake on economic development. Intellectual stagnation inevitably bred stagnation in deeds.

The Party has drawn the proper conclusions and has set a clear objective: to carry out large-scale measures improving the entire sytem of administration so as to substantially heighten its efficiency, focus it on a cardinal acceleration of scientific and technological progress, on an all-out mobilisation of the human factor. This objective has been thoroughly and profoundly substantiated in the Political Report of the Central Committee to the 27th Congress of the CPSU, which defined the cardinal line of our actions. Relying on the immutable principle of democratic centralism, we must follow this line, and continue consolidating and improving the centralised plan-governed guidance of the economy — socialism's great gain and essential advantage. In this matter, too, it is apparent that we have "not lived up to" and will never live up to the hopes of bourgeois ideologists that we will depart from that fundamental principle. At the same time, the Party will resolutely work for giving associations and enterprises more leeway, for heightening their responsibility for the end results and for developing cost accounting in depth. The vast scale of the economy and the diversification of inter-sectoral and regional ties also demand an optimum combination of sectoral and territorial administration and an improvement of the organisational structures.

In recent years important steps have been taken in this respect. A broader than ever search for and testing of more effective forms of administration, coupled with the introduction of innovations that have proved their worth, has become a typical feature of our economic life. We began by extending the rights and responsibilities of enterprises and associations — the level at which material values are produced and all management threads are intertwined. Here, the shortcomings of the economic mechanism were especially noticeable. The absence of a close linkage between the interests of work collectives and the end results of their work held down their initiative and enterprise and did not stimulate them to use the latent reserves of production. To avoid the mistakes made in the past, new methods are elaborated with an eye to the specificity of the particular economic branches. All this enables us to determine the merits and demerits of the new methods more conclusively, to perfect these methods, and extend the sphere of their use phase by phase.

During the 12th Five-Year Plan period we will have to persevere in developing an integrated system of administration, to consistently adjust the elements of the economic mechanism and look for more effective forms and methods of planning, stimulating and organising production.

One of the most important tasks in these five years is to introduce new methods of management in all branches of the economy. To date, enterprises accounting for half the industrial output, the entire communications system, the services industry, and some transportation enterprises, are operating along the new lines. From 1987, all industrial and transportation enterprises will operate on these principles. Simultaneously, within the shortest possible time, we must also complete the reorganisation of the management of the agro-industrial complex, create the prerequisites for substantially promoting economic methods, and for a broad introduction of truly cost-accounting relations on collective and state farms, at enterprises and associations.

As noted earlier, the management of the building industry calls for most urgent improvements. Here we must begin an experimental verification of the new planning methods and of elements of the economic mechanism this year, so as to subsequently spread them to the entire industry. The whole range of issues related to the organisation of management in capital construction calls for thorough study in the light of the tasks facing the country.

To promote cost accounting is especially important if we want to further improve the economic mechanism and comprehensively elaborate all its elements. A close and rigid dependence shoud be established between the end results achieved by the enterprises and associations and the funds they allocate for the development of production, remuneration of labour, material incentives for the personnel, for the satisfaction of their social needs. The idea is that these funds should increasingly determine all aspects of the life of enterprises: production as well as social.

For this purpose, we are setting the following tasks: first, to make the fund for production development the basic source of technical retooling and modernisation; second, to pursue the line for improving housing and other social and living conditions increasingly out of funds earned by the work collectives; third, to tie more closely the earnings of every worker to his or her personal contribution to the end results; fourth, to completely stop all channels that make it possible to pay for the mismanagement of some with the good results of others; fifth, to secure a further expansion of the sphere of contractual relationships and establish strict responsibility of enterprises for meeting their commitments to consumers. And, lastly, a most important thing: to stop petty supervision and interference of superior bodies in the lawful rights of work collectives, to enable the latter to find the optimum ways of fulfilling their plans. This is what full-scale cost accounting amounts to in practice. Precisely these economic conditions will inescapably require that enterprises and associations make the maximum use of the production potential, of the achievements of science and technology, that they economise on resources to the utmost, and that they react flexibly and promptly to the consumers' needs.

We must work consistently to improve cost accounting, and transfer enterprises to self-financing and self-sufficiency. These principles are now being comprehensively verified at the Volzhsky car works and the Sumy Research and Production Association. The results obtained there are good. We must follow this path energetically.

Developing the system of economic norms is especially important in improving the new methods of management. The norms must be set for the entire five-year period and give work collectives confidence that efficient work is sure to be rewarded materially and morally. Poor results, on the other hand, will affect the entire collective. The most dangerous thing here is to violate the principle of the stability of norms. Unfortunately, this does happen. Such practices undermine the cost accounting foundations and must, therefore, be most firmly combated.

It should be stressed that economic norms are a promising instrument of plan-governed management. They flexibly combine centralisation in economic management with the use of commodity-money relations and the law of value. It is important that central economic bodies, ministries and enterprises should learn to use them to the full extent. The sphere in which they are applied will have to be expanded in view of accumulated experience, the relationships between the state enterprises and the budget will have to be put on a normative basis.

The policy of extending the rights of enterprises that has been built into the new economic mechanism will not yield the desired effect unless its principles are applied at all levels of production, right down to the team and work place. This calls for an organic linkage of cost accounting at associations and enterprises with the development of the contractual form of organising and remunerating labour. That will offer greater scope to the creativity and initiative of the masses, the collectivist principles of production will be promoted, and people's involvement in the common cause will be brought home to them more clearly, thereby implementing Lenin's behest that every worker should feel "that he is not only the master of his own factory but that he is also a representative of the country", that he feels his responsibility.

the Report of the CPSU Central Committee treats in a new, principled way the development of democratic methods in management, the question of increasing the working people's immediate participation in the affairs of enterprises, a fuller and more effective application of the USSR Law on Work Collectives. We cannot expect the economic mechanism to function effectively without the active and creative participation of work collectives in drafting and implementing economic and social development plans, and resolving all issues related to the life of enterprises. That is why it is essential to find new collectivist forms for the working people's participation in management alongside the existing ones. As is pointed out in the Report, councils of work collectives could be one such effective form. Party, trade union, Komsomol and other public organisations must have their say in promoting the democratic principles of management.

In the recent past, underestimation of the role of

organisational structures in raising economic efficiency was a major shortcoming interfering with the work of improving management. In recent years the establishment of production associations was unjustifiably retarded, and they have failed to become the main form of organisation in a large number of industries. The process has to be given fresh impulse. We must also be bolder in forming large-scale intersectoral associations, which provide for effective specialisation and cooperation free from departmental partitions.

A new approach is needed to the role and functions of ministries. The content and style of their work, like their organisational structures, were shaped to serve the old, mainly administrative, methods of management. Considering the introduction of economic methods of management and the extension of the rights of enterprises and associations, ministries will have to be substantially restructured. In the interests of production, part of their former functions will have to be turned over to the work collectives, needless everyday routine abandoned, greater confidence placed in enterprises.

In the present conditions, ministries should concentrate mainly on charting the strategy of scientific and technological progress in the industry concerned and its development prospects, raising the general standard of economic work, and, in the final analysis, fully meeting society's needs for products. To these ends we must also radically improve the organisational system of sectoral administration, and, as a rule, adopt a bi-level scheme. Elaboration of such schemes in ministries of the engineering complex has already been completed, and it should be speeded up in all the other branches.

Ministries are faced with no easy tasks. And success depends in many ways on how organically they are integrated in the new system of management, and on how quickly they adapt themselves psychologically to the needs of the times.

The responsibility borne by our central economic bodies for making the economic mechanism more effective is exceedingly high. They are, indeed, the executors of the fundamental principles of Party policy.

It is no secret, however, that all too often in their practical activity, in screeds of written instructions and recommendations of methods, the substance of the issues is distorted, giving way to departmentalism and undermining vital undertakings. This evokes legitimate dissatisfaction locally. Such practices must be rooted out once and for all, and the letter and spirit of the Party decisions must be strictly observed.

The success of the ongoing restructuring of the economic mechanism largely depends on the USSR State Planning Committee. It must bring its activity in line with the new demands, emphasise the comprehensive approach to the key tasks, and bear full responsibility for a balanced and effective growth of the economy. It is also essential to rebuild the structure of the USSR State Planning Committee in this spirit, so as to concentrate its activity on promising economic problems, above all on shaping the national economic, intersectoral and regional proportions.

Responsible tasks are also facing the USSR State Supplies Committee. It will have to restructure its work in order to measure up to the needs of the new economic mechanism, and introduce effective forms of supply and marketing, including wholesale trade.

We expect bold and resolute action from the USSR Ministry of Finance. In recent years, the role of finances has weakened in economic affairs, and so has the work to make the economy more efficient. More, in a number of cases the finance and credit mechanism is holding back progressive changes. Substantial modifications are needed here to concentrate it on securing the expenditure-free tendency of developing production.

The work of the USSR State Bank and the USSR Construction Bank (Stroibank), too, should be revised to meet the new demands. At present, credits are highly ineffective. The conditions that would prompt enterprises and organisations, collective and state farms to use credits rationally, increase profitability, and settle accounts with the state in time and completely, have not yet been created. The banks must stand guard over the interests of the state and at the same time promote the initiative and economic enterprise of work collectives in every possible way.

The intensification of the economy heightens the role of prices as dependable gauges of the effectiveness of expenditures and of the results of economic activity, as effective stimuli of scientific and technological progress and of raising the quality of products. And the State Committee for Prices has a big part to play here. It must resolve the problems that have piled up in this field more quickly and more competently. The work concerning retail prices, too, must conform to the objectives of our social policy.

Of late, as we know, new managing bodies have been established for large economic complexes, such as the USSR State Agro-Industrial Committee and the Engineering Bureau. Their structure and functions are different, reflecting the specificity of either complex. As experience accumulates, it is expedient to further improve the guidance of groups of interconnected and related branches.

More attention will have to be devoted to a flexible combination of sectoral and territorial control. In so doing, we should not hesitate to give local Soviets more rights in economic planning and management, especially in such industries and spheres which concern the daily needs of the working people.

The improvements in management and the economic mechanism, coupled with the greater scientific weight of decision-making, are setting new and high demands on economists. They have a big debt to pay to the country. We expect them to produce effective theoretical studies and concrete practical recommendations.

In short, Comrades, hard work lies in store for us in the 12th Five-Year Plan period: we must restructure all the links of the economic mechanism. As we do this, we must see to it that the existing structures and forms of management organically develop into qualitatively new ones measuring up to the present-day tasks. This process should ensure a steady growth of production and its higher efficiency. This is an important matter and must be in the focus of attention and under the constant control of the central economic bodies, ministries and Party organisations. And it must be dealt with every day, perseveringly, preventing formalism and snags, and not retreating in the face of arising difficulties, as was sometimes the case in the past.

Of all the dangers along this road, the biggest one is red

tape. Creating the appearance of work, taking cover behind hollow rhetoric, bureaucracy may hold back the improvement of the economic mechanism, dampen independence and initiative, and erect barriers to what is new.

An urgent problem on which depends the success of the restructuring of the system of control and the methods of management is the professional training of our personnel. Here, economic education is an indispensable and essential element in training people of all professions.

We must work out an effective system for the economic education of workers and engineers, so that all of them can competently and knowledgeably evaluate the economic aspect of technical solutions. We should therefore seriously revise the character and content of all forms of education, including the higher schools of economics and economic faculties. Leading economists, both researchers and practicians, must be called in to do so. Lastly, a well-considered system embracing all levels of management is needed for retraining specialists in economics.

Especially high demands are set by modern-day economics on captains of production. It is necessary to cultivate up-to-date economic thinking among our managers — a high degree of professionalism, socialist initiative, the ability to see far ahead, to be educators and organisers within the work collective. The indispensable features of the present-day manager are his Party maturity and adherence to principle, undeviating implementation of the Party line, and impeccable moral qualities. They are essential if our constructive plans are to be carried into effect.

The tasks involved in improving the entire system of management are highly important not only economically, but also politically. That is why their implementation must be constantly controlled and guided by the Party organisations. Profound and concrete analysis of social and economic processes, perseverance in carrying out the Party's economic policy, the proper placing and education of economic executives, and readiness to support what is new and progressive — these are the areas where the Party's guidance of the economy must be concentrated and strengthened above all.

5. Foreign Economic Ties

Comrades, the Party's policy of accelerating the country's social and economic development sets high demands on our foreign economic activity. We hold that in the modern world, active development of economic, scientific and technical ties and participation in the international division of labour are vitally necessary. We consider this an important means of maintaining and strengthening peaceful, good-neighbourly relations among states, and of rendering mutual assistance in resolving national economic problems.

An entirely new situation can be created for international economic cooperation and its intensive growth in the interests of all countries if the Soviet programme of phased elimination of nuclear weapons by the year 2000 and the other peaceful proposals contained in the Political Report of the CPSU Central Committee are carried into effect. Disarmament would avert the threat of mankind's destruction and release tremendous material and intellectual resources for economic development. Faithful to the Leninist peace policy, the Soviet Union is sparing no effort to improve the international situation, and to maintain and strengthen relations of equitable cooperation with all countries irrespective of their social system. Our Party and the Soviet State will not be forced off this course by either threats from the imperialist forces or attempts to divert the Geneva talks from the main goal.

Accordingly, the draft Guidelines envisage a considerable expansion of foreign economic ties. They will be concentrated on the priorities, orientated on scientific and technological progress, and used to a greater extent for attaining social goals.

Cooperation with the fraternal socialist countries will be, as it has always been, the determining element. In the immediate future, pursuant to the decisions of the CMEA Economic Summit, a big step forward is to be made in building up socialist integration and developing it in depth on the basis of broad cooperation and specialisation of production. This is opening up new prospects for the further comprehensive expansion of economic ties between fraternal countries, speeding up the accomplishment of our common task of intensification and increasing our economic and technical invulnerability in the face of imperialist actions.

Consistent implementation of the Comprehensive Programme for the Scientific and Technological Progress of the CMEA Member-Countries up to the Year 2000 will be the core of all this work. The emphasis in integration activities is now shifting to joint utilization of the latest scientific and technical achievements, and to the development of extensive cooperation in all branches of the national economy, primarily in the manufacture of the modern types of machines and equipment. It is with this in view that our central planning and economic agencies, as well as ministries and departments must organise their foreign economic activity. Certainly, much will also depend on the improvement of the work of the Council for Mutual Economic Assistance, that collective organisation of the socialist countries.

The recently completed coordination of the national economic plans of the CMEA countries for 1986-1990 shows that a good amount of work will be accomplished already in the current five-year period. The in-depth development of integration processes calls for a creative, innovative approach. The old, habitual forms that took shape at the time of extensive development cannot secure any dynamic growth of cooperation. It is necessary therefore to find new approaches, decisively to switch over to direct interaction between enterprises and branches of the economy, develop direct economic ties, and set up joint associations, design bureaus and laboratories. A start has been made, and a number of joint research and production associations have been formed. These are only the beginnings of new forms of integration. But they are the future.

The Guidelines envisage a further consolidation of economic ties also with other socialist countries. Trade with the People's Republic of China is to increase considerably.

The Soviet Union will continue to develop cooperation with Asian, African and Latin American countries. Our wide-ranging assistance contributes to the formation and development of their national economies, helping them to overcome the colonial aftermath, and to move ahead along the road of economic and social progress. The USSR has stable, long-term relations with many of them, as with India, for example, and some other countries. And these ties are becoming increasingly beneficial for all concerned. Our policy of supporting developing states, which has become an important factor for restructuring international economic relations on a just and democratic basis, will be continued, especially with regard to the socialist-oriented countries.

Faithful to its policy of peaceful coexistence, the Soviet Union favours cooperation with the developed capitalist states. Here we see considerable potentialities. And that applies to practically all types of relations — commercial, scientific, technical, finance and credits, and so on. As known, cooperation is a two-way street. Here, mutual interest must be strictly considered, and all restrictions, boycotts and embargoes orchestrated by the USA must be completely renounced. In the modern world, economic relations can only be based on equal rights, trust, and strict observance of mutual agreements. To act contrary to this, subordinating commercial and economic ties to unseemly political aims is tantamount to trying to hold up world progress. Historical experience shows that such attempts hold no promise whatever. With this in view the Political Report of the CPSU Central Committee has set forth a new proposal — to call, in the future, a World Congress on Economic Security to discuss all that encumbers international economic relations.

Foreign trade is making a tangible and ever increasing contribution to the development of our economy. There is now practically no branch that has been left out of the sphere of foreign economic relations. But it is impossible to advance rapidly by traditional routes. The first thing to do is to change the raw materials orientation of our exports, and to increase the share of the manufacturing industry in them. This takes time, of course, but work in this area must get off the ground already in the 12th Five-Year Plan period. The ministries, associations and enterprises have to be orientated towards building up the country's export potential, and to raising the quality and competitiveness of machines and equipment, and other manufactured goods. Foreign currency spending must also be strictly regulated. Our import policy is called upon to actively help accelerate scientific and technological progress.

The foreign economic relations agencies, too, should restructure their work in the spirit of the new demands. There are still major flaws and shortcomings in the work of the Ministry of Foreign Trade and the State Committee for Foreign Economic Relations, which are being eliminated rather slowly. It is essential that these agencies should have closer contacts with the ministries and enterprises, and that they should search for forms of coordinating their interests with the demands of the foreign market and be active participants rather than mere middlemen in carrying out national economic tasks.

Social Development and Improvement of the People's Well-being in the 12th Five-Year Plan Period

Comrade Delegates, the growth of the economy and its higher efficiency, as envisaged in the 12th Five-Year Plan, form a reliable basis for a substantial advance in carrying out the programme guidelines of the CPSU — to raise the standard of living of Soviet people to a qualitatively new level and secure a steady improvement of their working and living conditions. The Party links these objectives organically with the harmonious development of the individual and the promotion of the working people's creative initiative. That is the substance of a forceful social policy in conditions of accelerated social progress in the USSR. The essential demand is to implement the principle of social justice, and the socialist distribution of goods and benefits to the fullest.

Accordingly, special attention in the 12th Five-Year Plan is devoted to issues whose solution helps maximally to improve the quality of the life and activity of Soviet people, and to increase the labour contribution of every citizen to the common cause.

The interests of both social and economic development call, above all, for serious changes in the conditions, character and content of labour. Among the various requirements of the members of society, the need for meaningful and creative labour is coming more and more to the fore. In the new five-year period we must secure a breakthrough in carrying out the urgent task of reducing unskilled manual labour. The scale and rate of its reduction must increase by at least 100 to 200 per cent.

The accelerated modernisation of the production apparatus, the mechanisation, automation and electronisation of production, the overall drive for technical retooling, must be directed towards improving the conditions and enriching the content of labour. Systematic certification of work places and scientific organisation of labour are called upon to promote this objective.

We must also bear in mind the other side of the question. The high educational and professional standard of the Soviet worker makes it imperative to create proper conditions in production. The present-day worker will no longer agree to operate obsolete machinery and use old techniques. And managers must reckon with this.

It is a task of tremendous social and economic significance to make the system of remuneration more effective. The elements of equalization that have increased of late, and serious shortcomings in setting work quotas and establishing wages and salaries are undermining the role of these incentives, and are holding down the growth of productivity. We cannot put up with this situation. The earnings of every working person must be strictly adequate to the results of his or her work. The strict relationship between the growth of emoluments and the growth of productivity is imperative for the modern-day economy, and we will insist on its being observed without fail.

It is in this context that it has been determined how to carry out the major undertaking — raising basic rates and salaries, as envisaged in the Guidelines. We deem it essential to introduce new basic rates and salaries in the various fields of material production within a short term: practically in just five years. They are to be raised by an average of 25 to 30 per cent. And perhaps the most important thing is that we have worked out a fundamentally new, active approach to the question of funds for it. Now, the funds required for this must be earned chiefly by the work collectives through the growth of production, higher production efficiency, mobilization of internal resources, and better organisation of labour and work quotas setting.

This approach makes the introduction of new basic rates and salaries directly dependent on better performance and higher labour productivity at enterprise level. It relies on the experience that many industrial and other enterprises have gained working in the new economic conditions. This method has been experimentally tested on the Byelorussian Railway where the increase in basic rates and salaries is financed out of internal resources obtained through extensive preparatory economic and organisational work, and better use of machinery.

Considerable funds are earmarked for increasing the wages and salaries of people employed in non-productive fields. Next year, as envisaged by the school reform, the transfer of all those employed in public education to new terms of remuneration will be completed. There will be phased increases in the salaries of doctors and other medical personnel. The basic rates and salaries of some categories of employees at cultural institutions and higher educational establishments will also be raised in the 12th Five-Year Plan period. These measures are a concrete expression of the Party's concern for the further growth of the socio-cultural sphere.

The measures that are to be carried out in the field of earnings will make it possible to raise the average monthly wage and salary to 215-220 roubles by the end of the current five years.

Remuneration for collective-farm work will rise more rapidly. According to the planned increase in labour productivity it will rise on an average to 180 roubles a month. Plus the earnings that collective farmers derive from their individual small holdings, their real incomes will, in effect, level up with those of factory and office workers. Along with the greater mechanisation of labour and the priority growth of the rate of construction of dwellings and cultural and community facilities in the rural areas, this will be an important step forward in overcoming the basic distinctions between town and country, a programme objective of the CPSU.

Along with the consolidation of the principle of distribution according to work, we will continue to consistently build up the social consumption funds, which play an exceptional role in the life of Soviet people. They will go up considerably in these five years, and will amount to over 600 roubles per capita in 1990.

In its social policy the Party has always devoted special attention to improving conditions for the upbringing of the rising generation. In the 12th Five-Year Plan period the state's assistance to families with children will increase still more. The introduction a few years ago of paid leave for working mothers to look after their infants until the age of one has begun to yield a fairly good socio-demographic effect. Considering this factor, and also the wishes of citizens expressed during the discussion of the draft Guidelines, it has been found desirable to extend this leave by another six months. It is also intended to lengthen the prenatal leave and the paid time off to look after sick children, and to introduce free medicines for children up to three years of age.

It is of major socio-economic importance to accomplish the vital task of fully meeting the demand for pre-school childcare centres within the next few years. The objective is quite attainable. Where this issue receives due attention, it is being successfully resolved. The heads of ministries and departments, as well as local bodies, should keep the question of building kindergartens and infant nurseries under constant control.

Large funds will be allocated for improving the pension scheme, increasing society's aid to war and labour veterans, and to the families of fallen soldiers. It is planned to substantially increase the number, and improve the work, of hostels for the aged. Progressive forms of servicing disabled citizens will be used on a broader scale.

The planned increases in wages and salaries and expansion of social consumption funds in the 12th Five-Year Plan period will bring about visible changes in the condition and standard of life of large segments of society. The countrywide wage and salary increases, as well as increases in pensions and allowances, will raise the incomes of more than half the country's population.

This will benefit nearly twice as many people as in the past five years. By the end of the current five years more than 50 per cent of all families will have an average monthly per capita income of more than 125 roubles. There will be practically no families with a monthly per capita income of 50 roubles or less.

In the 12th Five-Year Plan period, special emphasis is on the steady consolidation of the material and technical basis of the socio-cultural sphere. The school reform envisages a 40 per cent increase in classroom capacities, and better conditions for the training and educational process. It is also planned to reorganise specialised secondary and higher education. The reorganisation must be aimed at an all-round improvement in the quality of specialist training, closer ties between higher educational establishments and production, and their more active participation in the development of science and technology. All this, too, calls for a further consolidation of the material base of higher education.

Much has to be done to effectively improve the work of health institutions, enhance their preventive orientation, and gradually go over to periodic medical checkups of the entire population. The building of outpatient clinics and the output of medical instruments and accessories are to be increased about 50 per cent. The planned environmental protection measures, too, will be important for the health of people.

Large-scale construction of cultural and sports facilities is planned. In these five years, for example, it is planned to build more than 500 district houses of culture and more than 5,500 village clubs. As a result, there will be a house of culture in every district centre.

In short, we are planning to take an important step towards attaining the Party's objective of raising the socio-cultural sphere to a qualitatively new level within the 12th Five-Year Plan period.

If we want to accomplish this, we must renounce the view that prevails among certain executives, including those in planning bodies, that building socio-cultural institutions is a matter of minor importance. It will be admitted that the 1986 allocations for the development of some of the sectors of the socio-cultural sphere are below the average annual sum for the five years. This must be set right when finalising the Five-Year Plan.

And, of course, the funds earmarked for these purposes have to be fully and effectively used everywhere. It is not easy to obtain these funds. And we must use them carefully. Byelorussia, Lithuania, and many regions of the Russian Federation have managed matters so well that the plans for commissioning public education and health institutions are not merely being fulfilled, but also overfulfilled. At the ame time some of the republics and cities systematically fail to meet their plans of socio-cultural construction year after year. Here are two concrete examples. In Ashkhabad, the second wing of a clinical hospital has been going up for all of nine years. Its completion is now scheduled for 1989, and this despite the fixed time limits of three and a half years. A new wing of the Krasnoyarsk territorial hospital is going up at an intolerably slow rate. This is most outrageous, because the project is being financed partly from the earnings of All-Union Communist Subbotniks. Similar facts are known in the Georgian and Uzbek republics, Khabarovsk Territory, and Perm and other regions.

The housing problem is an object of the Party's constant concern. The results achieved here are considerable. Today, more than 80 per cent of the families living in urban areas have separate flats. People in the villages are also much better off as regards modern housing. But, all the same, housing is still an acute social problem. In the coming five years, it is planned to erect new housing with a total of 565-570 million square metres of living space. Considerable resources will be allocated for improving towns and villages, expanding utilities, services, amenities, and public transport facilities.

The acute housing problem calls for all-out mobilisation of energy and resources. Most local bodies, as well as ministries and departments, are doing just that. But there are examples of another kind. In the Armenian Republic, for instance, there is an annual shortfall in house-building, although the need for housing is great, and in some cities, moreover, water supplies are inadequate. At the same time, the impermissible practice of building contractors was busy with 12 projects that were not in the plan, including some that were of no special importance. Regrettably, such practices take place also in other regions. They must be nipped in the bud.

In the Party's social policy, priority importance is attached to the fullest possible satisfaction of the growing effective demand of the people. It is no exaggeration to say that today this is one of the most topical issues. Directly connected with this is the strengthening of material incentives of labour, rational use of free time, the moods of Soviet people, and the elimination of negative phenomena engendered by shortages.

First in line is the objective of improving food supplies, especially supplies of meat and dairy products, vegetables, and fruit. This is the aim of the Food Programme of the USSR. The attainment of the production targets which it sets for 1990 will make it possible to bring about far-reaching changes in the structure and quality of the nation's diet—the biggest changes in the past few five-year periods.

Progressive changes must also be achieved in the consumption of manufactured goods. The supply of these goods has gone up visibly in recent years, with many items having already saturated the market. Now, a more involved problem, that of quality and assortment, is moving into the fore. The Comprehensive Programme for the Development of Consumer Goods Production and Services indicates the ways of restructuring commodity output. An active role in resolving the problem is assigned to trade. The USSR Ministry of Trade and the Central Union of Cooperative Societies are too slow in eliminating shortcomings and, all too often, take an unprincipled and passive posture towards enterprises that put out low-quality goods, manoeuvre too slowly with commodity stocks, and fail to study the consumer demand with due care. The standard of trade and services is still impermissibly low. While dealing with questions related to the expansion of the assortment and output of fashionable goods, we must not, of course, unjustifiably reduce the production of inexpensive but quality commodities, above all for children and people of advanced age.

It is only right to stress that the task of satisfying effective demand is of special significance at this time, when the Party has mounted a relentless offensive against hard drinking and alcoholism. The policy of sharply reducing output and sales of liquor will be firmly pursued in the future as well. This will help to change the structure of consumption for the better, and will be reflected in the Five-Year and annual Plans.

On the whole, it is envisaged to increase retail trade by nearly one-third in these five years (excluding sales of liquor).

Paid services are to be developed along new lines, on a large scale, and energetically. Throughout the past few years, paid services accounted for a mere 10 per cent of the population's overall expenditure. Being far below the needs of people, this deforms the structure of demand, shifting it to commodities. An up-to-date highly developed sphere of services encompassing everyday life, recreation, tourism, and people's leisure — in effect, a new branch of the economy — is to be built within a short period of time. A breakthrough in this important sphere is to be achieved in the 12th Five-Year Plan period. The volume of paid services is to go up by 30 to 40 per cent.

The main aspect in improving services is the substantial expansion of the network of specialised enterprises and organisations. But this will take both time and resources. To get things off the ground rapidly it has been decided to enlist enterprises of all the economic branches, regardless of their type of activity, for providing services to the public. But this work is not developing successfully everywhere so far. And it is incumbent on the local bodies, the Soviet of People's Deputies, to take a most active part in it.

Such, Comrades, are the main tasks involved in promoting the well-being, improving the working and living conditions as well as the life-style of Soviet people in the 12th Five-Year Plan period. Once fulfilled, they will doubtlessly consolidate the socialist way of life still more, organically combining the improvement of the material well-being with the progress of culture and the all-out development of the creative activity of the population.

Concerned with improving all aspects of the life of the people, the Party is raising to a new level the importance of everlasting moral values and ideals which will exercise an increasing influence on the development of the Soviet citizen as a builder of communism.

Comrade Delegates,

Each passing day of the 27th Congress shows even more graphically and impressively the grandeur of what is projected by the Party, the grandeur of the tasks set in the Central Committee's Political Report and the other documents of the Congress. The ideas and decisions of the Congress are models of the creative use of Marxism-Leninism in this special period, which is for us a time of profound change and vigorous action. And I can say with complete certainty that their transformative and constructive force will continuously increase, exercising a revolutionising effect on all aspects of the life of our society.

The question now is to carry out our plans with all the resolve, energy, and perseverance, to mount a battle for the practical fulfilment of our set tasks by relying on the constructive creativity of the masses, on the nationwide socialist emulation movement. They are noble tasks, consonant with the vital interests of our people, with their ideals and peaceful aspirations.

To fulfil them is to ensure a further strengthening of the power and prosperity of our Homeland.

To fulfil them is to make the life of the Soviet people, of every Soviet family, better than it was.

To fulfil them is to consolidate the positions of socialism and world peace, and to protect our planet from nuclear catastrophe, to safeguard peace.

It is quite safe to say that the working people of our country, rallied closely round their Leninist Party, will, with a high sense of responsibility and aware of the demands of the time, do everything they can for the successful fulfilment of the historic decisions of the 27th Congress of the CPSU.

RESOLUTION OF THE 27TH CONGRESS OF THE CPSU

On the Guidelines for the Economic and Social Development of the USSR for 1986-1990 and for the Period Ending in 2000

Having heard and discussed the report of the Chairman of the USSR Council of Ministers, Comrade Nikolai Ryzhkov, on the Guidelines for the Economic and Social Development of the USSR for 1986-1990 and for the Period Ending in 2000, the 27th Congress of the Communist Party of the Soviet Union notes that the draft Guidelines are in accord with the provisions of the new edition of the Programme of the CPSU, the Party's general course of accelerating the socio-economic development of the country, and the tasks of intensification of the national economy on the basis of scientific and technological progress, of ensuring a steady improvement in the people's well-being and of maintaining the country's defence capability at the proper level.

The 27th Congress of the Communist Party of the Soviet Union resolves:

1. To approve the Guidelines for the Economic and Social Development of the USSR for 1986-1990 and for the Period Ending in 2000.

2. For the Council of Ministers of the USSR to draft, in accordance with the Guidelines, the State Plan for the Economic and Social Development of the USSR for 1986-1990, with assignments specified for each year of the five-year period, for the ministries and departments of the USSR, for the Union Republics and for the major economic areas, and to submit it to the Supreme Soviet of the USSR for consideration in May 1986.

To provide, in the Five-Year Plan, for carrying out the assignments and measures established in the Guidelines to raise the economic growth rates and efficiency and to further improve the Soviet people's living standards. In drawing up the Five-Year Plan, to consider the proposals made at the 27th Congress of the CPSU, during the election campaign in the Party and during the countrywide discussion of the draft new edition of the Programme of the CPSU and the draft Guidelines.

3. The 27th Congress of the CPSU believes that competent finalisation of the new Five-Year Plan and organisation of its efficient implementation is a major economic and political task of all Party, government, trade union, YCL, and economic organisations.

It is imperative to ensure, in the 12th Five-Year Plan period, a radical improvement in the work, to mobilise our resources and possibilities more fully, and to set into motion all the potentialities for the definite fulfilment of the charted plans. Giving broad rein to the creative initiative of the masses and strengthening discipline and order, to step up the rates of advance along all the directions of socio-economic development.

The Congress expresses the firm conviction that, under the Communist Party's leadership, the Soviet people will score fresh successes in building communism and in consolidating the might of our socialist Motherland.

SELECT STATISTICAL APPENDIX — D

SOCIAL STATISTICS

POPULATION
(million people)

Total, as of January 1, 1985	Urban	Rural	Men	Women
276.3	180.2	96.1	129.6	146.7

SOCIAL COMPOSITION OF THE POPULATION, INCLUDING NON-WORKING MEMBERS OF THE FAMILY
(per cent)

	1939	1959	1984
Workers	33.7	50.2	61.5
Coll. farmers and coop. craftsmen	47.2	31.4	12.5
Office employees	16.5	18.1	26.0

SOCIAL COMPOSITION OF THE COMMUNIST PARTY
(per cent)

Workers	44.1
Collective farmers	12.4
Office employees	43.5

MEMBERSHIP OF PUBLIC ORGANISATIONS

Trade unions	134,900,000
Young Communist League	42,000,000
League of Red Cross societies	116,000,000
Society of inventors and rationalisers	13,000,000
Scientific and technical societies	11,000,000
Union of writers	9,000
Union of artists	18,000
Union of architects	17,000
Union of film makers	6,000
Union of composers	2,000
Union of journalists	76,000

NUMBER OF PHYSICIANS

Year	No. thousand
1965	554
1970	668
1980	997
1984	1,236

NUMBER OF STUDENTS
(million people)

	1981-82	1982-83	1983-84	1984-85
General education secondary schools	44.3	44.3	44.5	44.6
Specialised secondary schools	4.5	4.5	4.5	4.5
Vocational schools	3.9	4.0	4.0	4.1
Institutions of higher learning	5.2	5.3	5.3	5.3
Refresher courses	44.7	47.5	47.0	47.5
Total	102.6	105.6	105.3	106.0

NUMBER OF RESEARCH WORKERS

Year	No. (million persons)
1965	0.7
1970	0.9
1980	1.4
1984	1.5

INCOMES

AVERAGE MONTHLY WAGES AND SALARIES AND PAYMENTS FROM PUBLIC CONSUMPTION FUNDS

Year	Average Monthly Wages and Salaries (roubles)	Payments from Public Consumption Funds (roubles per capita)
1970	122.0	263
1980	168.9	441
1982	177.3	495*
1984	185.0	508

* refers to the year 1983.

AGRICULTURE

AREA UNDER CROPS
(million hectares)

Cereals	119.6
Fodder crops	69.9
Industrial crops	13.9
Potatoes and other vegetables	9.2

AVERAGE ANNUAL GRAIN PRODUCTION
(million tons)

Year	Production
1966-70	167.6
1971-75	181.6
1976-80	205.0
1981-85 (planned)	238-243

OUTPUT OF FARM PRODUCE
(million tons)

	1960	1970	1980	1984
Raw cotton	4.3	6.9	9.9	8.6
Sugar Beet	57.7	78.9	79.6	85.3
Sunflower	4.0	6.1	4.7	4.5
Potatoes	84.4	98.8	66.9	85.3
Other vegetables	16.6	21.2	25.9	30.7

LIVESTOCK
(million head)

	1960	1970	1980	1984
Cattle	75.8	99.2	115.1	120.9
Pigs	58.7	67.5	73.9	77.8
Sheep and goats	140.3	143.4	143.7	148.9

OUTPUT OF LIVESTOCK PRODUCTS

	1960	1970	1980	1984
Meat (*slaughter weight, mln tons*)	8.7	12.3	15.1	16.7
Milk (*mln tons*)	61.7	83.0	90.6	97.6
Eggs (*thou mln*)	27.4	40.7	67.8	76.0
Wool (*thou tons*)	357	419	461	463

INDUSTRY & TRADE

AVERAGE DAILY OUTPUT

	1970	1975	1980	1984
Electric power (*mln kwh*)	2,030	2,845	3,535	4,078
Oil, including gas condensate (*thou tons*)	967	1,345	1,648	1,674
Natural gas (*mln cu m*)	542	793	1,189	1,605
Coal (*thou tons*)	1,710	1,921	1,957	1,946
Steel (*thou tons*)	318	387	404	421
Iron ore (*thou tons*)	540	644	669	675
Tractors (*units*)	1,256	1,508	1,516	1,561
Textiles (*mln sq m*)	24.3	27.3	29.4	32.1
Leather footwear (*thou pairs*)	1,860	1,913	2,030	2,086
TV sets (*thou units*)	18	19	21	25
Watches (*thou units*)	110	151	182	183

PRODUCTION OF ELECTRICITY, OIL, NATURAL GAS AND COAL

	1960	1970	1980	1984
Electricity (*thou mln kwh*)	292	741	1,294	1,493
Oil, including gas condensate (*mln tons*)	148	353	603	613
Gas (*thou mln cu m*)	45	198	435	547
Coal (*mln tons*)	510	624	716	712

LENGTH OF GAS PIPELINES
(in thousand kilometres)

Year	Length
1970	67.5
1975	98.8
1980	131
1983	155

PRODUCTION OF DURABLE GOODS
(million units)

	1960	1970	1980	1984
Motor cars	0.1	0.3	1.3	1.3
Radio sets and radiograms	4.2	7.8	8.5	9.4
TV sets	1.7	6.7	7.5	9.0
Refrigerators	0.5	4.1	5.9	5.7

FUTURE PROJECTIONS

	1985	1990	2000
Growth of the national income	100%	119-122%	nearly double
Real incomes of the population	100%	114%	160-180%
Growth of national income through higher labour productivity	75%	96%	100%
Labour productivity	100%	125%	230-250%
Reduction in power consumption per rouble of national income	7·1%	91.5%	100%

Source : Abel Aganbegian, *Make the Economy Responsive to Innovation.*

FOREIGN TRADE
(thousand million roubles)

	1960	1970	1980	1984
including :	10	22	94	140
export	5	11.5	50	75
import	5	10.5	44	65

Source : for all the tables :
Year Book USSR 86

(Published by Novosti Press Agency)